Prayin' to Be Set Free

Other titles in the *Real Voices, Real History*™ *Series*

My Folks Don't Want Me to Talk About Slavery
edited by Belinda Hurmence

Before Freedom, When I Just Can Remember
edited by Belinda Hurmence

We Lived in a Little Cabin in the Yard
edited by Belinda Hurmence

Mighty Rough Times, I Tell You
edited by Andrea Sutcliffe

On Jordan's Stormy Banks
edited by Andrew Waters

John F. Blair, Publisher
Winston-Salem, North Carolina

Prayin' to Be Set Free

Personal Accounts of Slavery in Mississippi

EDITED BY ANDREW WATERS

Published by John F. Blair, Publisher

*The paper in this book meets the guidelines
for permanence and durability of the
Committee on Production Guidelines for
Book Longevity of the Council on Library Resources.*

Library of Congress Cataloging-in-Publication Data
Prayin' to be set free : personal accounts of slavery in
Mississippi / edited by Andrew Waters.
p.   cm. — (Real voices, real history series)
ISBN 0-89587-256-0 (alk. paper)
1. Slaves—Mississippi—Biography. 2. Slaves—Mississippi—
Social conditions—19th century. 3. African Americans—
Mississippi—Interviews. 4. African Americans—Mississippi—
Social conditions—19th century. 5. Mississippi—Biography.
I. Title: Praying to be set free. II. Waters, Andrew, 1970–
III. Series

E445 M6 P73 2002
305.5'67'0922762—dc21
[B]   2001055368

Cover photograph courtesy of The Library of Congress
Title: Mississippi Negress hoeing cotton. She was born a slave "two years before the Surrender."
Photographer: Dorothea Lange for the Farm Security Administration
Design by Debra Long Hampton
Composition by The Roberts Group

For my hero, Robert Charles Waters

Contents

Introduction

Prior to working on this volume of Mississippi slave narratives, my primary experience with the African-Americans of that state was through the blues. I am a blues fan, and although my favorites are from the generation that gained prominence in the 1950s and 1960s—the great Mississippi Fred McDowell, the sublime Mississippi John Hurt, B. B. King, and others—I am familiar with that first generation of famous blues singers from the 1920s and 1930s, including Charlie Patton, Skip James, and Robert Johnson.

The comparison is useful for several reasons. The blues recordings from the Great Depression are often described as raw and intense, open and powerful. Certainly, there is none of the studio gimmickry in those records that we take for granted today, no hint of computers or political correctness. The words of the Mississippians in these narratives, all born under slavery, often possess that same raw, intense power.

"It sho' was terrible times," says James Lucas of his service with the Union army. "These old eyes of mine seen more people crippled and dead. I's even seen 'em saw off legs with hacksaws. I tell you, it ain't right, what I seen. It ain't right at all."

The life of Prince Johnson, who was approximately ninety when interviewed in Coahoma County, also has the makings of a blues song. "I expected to spend the rest of my days right there on the same place," he says of the 360-acre farm he purchased from a white man named Armstrong after the Civil War, "but you never can tell in this life what's going to happen. During the Cleveland administration, cotton went to a nickel a pound. That was the year I lost my land. Mr. Armstrong went broke, and I went right down with him. We was both plumb busted."

The early blues were marked by tales of violence, as are these narratives. Lizzie Williams, an eighty-eight-year-old former slave from Grenada County, gives this account: "I's seen nigger women that was fixin' to be confined [give birth] do somethin' the white folks didn't like. They would dig a hole in the ground just big 'nough for her stomach, make her lie face down, and whip her on the back to keep from hurtin' the child."

Susan Snow's narrative echoes another element of

the blues: the struggle with oneself. "When I come to Meridian, I cut loose," says the eighty-seven-year-old. "I's tellin' the truth! I's a woman, but I's a prodigal. I used to be a old drunkard. . . . The niggers called me 'Devil.' I was a devil 'til I got religion."

To say that the blues is about only pain and suffering is to stereotype the form unfairly, however. Anyone who has listened to those early recordings knows there is also joy in them—or if not joy, then exuberance and vitality. These narratives are no different. The happiest times are often recalled from childhood days. The following account by Belle Caruthers, charged with caring for her master's infant, is particularly poignant. "The baby had alphabet blocks to play with, and I learned my letters while she learned hers. . . . I found a hymn book one day and spelled out, 'When I Can Read My Title Clear.' I was so happy when I saw I could really read that I ran around telling all the other slaves."

Occasionally, the narratives also reveal some measure of contentment at the end of life, as is evident in this passage from Henri Necaise, who was 105 when interviewed at his home near Nicholson. "I did get me this little farm, forty acres, but I bought and paid for it myself. . . . This here house has been built for 52 years. I's still livin' in 'em. They's mine."

These Mississippi slave narratives and the first blues recordings share an element of timing as well as content. Robert Johnson made his seminal recordings in 1936 and

1937, approximately the same time the Federal Writers' Project was being created by the United States Works Progress (later Work Projects) Administration to provide employment to out-of-work writers, editors, and artists. In the South and a few scattered states including Ohio, Oklahoma, and Colorado, one of the Writers' Project's major undertakings was recording the memories of former slaves. A network of field workers was assigned the task of identifying and interviewing African-Americans who had lived under slavery. Most interviewees were in their eighties or nineties at the time. Some were even older. The former slaves were thus far more advanced in age than the young blues singers who were starting to gain national recognition in 1937 and 1938, the same period these narratives were recorded. But the world they inhabited and described was the same.

The material that resulted from these interviews was as rough as it was vast. In the age before tape recorders, workers were sent into the field with only a list of questions, pencils, and paper. The interviews were transcribed in longhand, then typed. Some were recorded in the first person with substantial effort to capture the subjects' tone and dialect. Others were more factual third-person accounts. Interviewers usually worked from a prepared list of questions from which they rarely strayed, even when doing so would have enriched the historical value of the content. Some narratives consisted of only brief snippets of information, the interviews cut short by approaching meals or zealous editors. Others were comprised of several different interviews conducted over a long period of time, with much of the same information revealed in each one. Numerous versions of the same interviews were common. The field workers' material was usually edited at least once by regional supervisors. The various versions—rough draft, first edit, second edit, etc.—were often stored in different places, making it almost impossible for later researchers to determine which version was the "official" one.

Despite these challenges and mistakes, the project was a resounding success. More than two thousand narratives were eventually collected from seventeen states and stored at the Library of Congress under the title *Slave Narratives: A Folk History of Slavery in the U.S. from Interviews with Former Slaves*. As impressive as that collection was—and is—thousands of interviews never made it to Washington, D.C. Some were lost. Others were archived to be edited at a later date that never came. Some were cut or completely suppressed because they were deemed untrue or because they depicted the ancestors of prominent white Southerners harshly.

For years, the narratives were a well-kept secret accessible only in the Rare Book Room of the Library of Congress or on microfilm for a $110 fee. In 1972, scholar George P. Rawick published a complete edition of the narratives grouped according to state. Titled *The American Slave: A Composite Autobiography,* this edition made the narratives widely available to the public for the first time. It also sparked a renewed interest in the material and led to the discovery of "lost" narratives in various state and local institutions. As a result, Rawick and his colleagues followed *The American Slave* with a ten-volume supplement published in 1979, compiled from narratives that were not originally submitted to the Library of Congress. A true labor of love, it contained thousands of accounts—including the majority of the narratives found in this collection—that otherwise might still be languishing in storerooms.

In the early 1980s, North Carolina writer Belinda Hurmence began researching the slave narratives for a novel. Finding the collection of rough drafts, duplicate versions, and third-person accounts unnecessarily intimidating, she decided to pare it down to North Carolina narratives that would be more accessible to the general public. Her 1984 book, *My Folks Don't Want Me to Talk about Slavery*, contained twenty-one narratives selected for their quality. Hurmence's criteria were that the narratives had to be first-person accounts and that they had to contain memories of life under slavery and recollections of the Civil War. The second criterion was necessary because many of those interviewed by the Federal Writers' Project were born just before the Civil War and had no clear memories of slavery. That first collection was followed by a similar South Carolina collection, *Before Freedom, When I Just Can Remember*, and a

Virginia collection, *We Lived in a Little Cabin in the Yard*.

This volume—like the other slave-narrative collections subsequently published in this series—adheres closely to Hurmence's successful formula. All of the narratives in *Prayin' to Be Set Free* are written in the first person, which captures these elderly Americans' human vitality in a way that third-person accounts cannot. Each former slave provides an account of life under slavery, and the majority tell about their experiences during the Civil War.

My job as editor was to pick close to thirty narratives that fit these criteria and best represented the life of former slaves in Mississippi. I tried to balance the accounts of males and females, so that the two sexes' very different experiences of slavery were represented fairly. I also tried to ensure that the narratives came from a variety of geographic locations, though readers will note that several narratives are from Meridian and Coahoma County. I was limited to a certain degree by the source material itself. The Federal Writers' Project worked out of regional offices, and areas close to the headquarters were canvassed better than areas farther afield. Some of the rural counties of the Delta and Piney Woods regions of the state, as well as the largely white counties of northeastern Mississippi, weren't represented in the source material at all.

The major editorial challenge in this collection was the issue of dialect. Dialect was employed heavily by the writers and editors of the Federal Writers' Project, presumably because they felt it was as important to pre-serve the subjects' way of talking as it was to preserve what they said. Unfortunately, the heavy use of dialect can make the narratives challenging to modern readers. I suppose it would have been possible to correct all the unusual spellings and abbreviations, but that did not seem the ideal solution, since the manner of speaking is part of the stories. Therefore, I attempted to balance these two issues, correcting obscure abbreviations and mis-spellings but leaving the unusual syntax intact. Obscure words are often interpreted within brackets, and edito-rial notes are employed to clarify confusing accounts. Many of these devices were added by the original inter-viewers and editors. I have also added my own when I felt it was necessary.

Though there were other challenges in preparing this book, they were easily outweighed by the quality of these accounts. Mississippi's deep connection to the slavery system makes this material particularly rich.

At the time the United States gained control of what is now Mississippi in 1798, the region's population, ex-cluding Native Americans, was barely 8,500. About 5,000 were whites and the remainder slaves. The ma-jority of the population lived in or near Natchez, the sole outpost of civilization. Mississippi was isolated— Natchez itself was accessible only by boat in the early days—but that quickly changed under American con-trol. White immigrants poured into the state, bringing with them a flood of slaves. By 1860, there were 436,631 slaves in Mississippi, according to the census. That same year, the state contained 353,901 white persons, of whom 30,943—or 8.75 percent—were listed in the census as slaveholders. That percentage may appear small, but as Charles Sackett Sydnor points out in his book *Slavery in Mississippi*, the slaveholders were typically heads of families of five or more. Assuming an average family size, Sydnor estimates that just under half of Mississippi's white population was involved in the ownership of slaves just before the Civil War.

Mississippi differed from the eastern slave states in several respects.

It was considered a slave buyer, as opposed to Virginia, Maryland, South Carolina, and other eastern seaboard states, which typically sold slaves to their western neighbors. This is reflected in several of the narratives. The former slaves rarely trace their Mississippi roots back more than one generation. Many recall coming to the state as children.

Up to and during the Civil War, Mississippi possessed a rough, frontier-type atmosphere and an economy given over almost entirely to cotton planting. In 1830, Mississippi produced 13 percent of the cotton grown in the United States. By 1849, that figure had risen to almost 19 percent. By 1859, it was just over 21 percent. Cotton plantations required tremendous amounts of labor, supplied by slaves. In times of economic prosperity, those plantations rendered huge profits to their white owners. Few blacks in Mississippi knew of life outside their own and neighboring plantations, which made the prospect of freedom both thrilling and daunting for many.

In 1937, a surprising number of former slaves remained alive in Mississippi. Estimates suggest there were approximately 20,000 of them. About 560 (2.8 percent) were noted in WPA materials, and 450 of these were actually interviewed. Many who have studied the entire collection of slave narratives consider the Mississippi interviews to be the most interesting. "The narratives from the State of Mississippi are colorful, interesting and most of them rich in description and color regarding slavery, plantation life, and the Civil War," wrote one evaluator. "They were by far the most valuable and important narratives that I accessed." Another wrote, "The Mississippi narratives . . . are among the best. They . . . are full of information about slavery told in the first person in a lively, interesting manner." It is my hope that you will have a similar reaction.

There are aspects of these accounts that modern readers may find puzzling, perhaps disturbing. Many memories in these pages reveal the brutal injustices of slavery, but just as many depict it fondly. "I guess slavery was wrong," says James Lucas, "but I 'members us had some mighty good times." Henri Necaise adds, "It ain't none of my business 'bout whether the niggers is better off free than slaves. I don't know 'cept 'bout me. I was better off then."

Please bear in mind that these interviews were conducted during the late 1930s. By that time, even the youngest of those born into slavery were well into their seventies, and most were much older. These elderly people had lived through slavery, the bloody Civil War, the turbulent Reconstruction period, the era of Jim Crow laws that sprang from Reconstruction, and World War I. Old age and economic depression were bringing what had already been tumultuous, hard lives to a difficult close. This perhaps makes it easier to understand why some of these former slaves viewed their days under slavery as pleasurable, even joyful.

The context of the interviews also played a role in the tone of the narratives. Most interviews were conducted by whites, and many scholars have suggested that the elderly blacks were simply practicing a lifelong habit of telling whites what they thought they wanted to hear. This may have been particularly true in Mississippi, where most of the interviews were conducted by white women upon whose goodwill the elderly blacks may have depended, directly or indirectly.

It is also quite possible that the interviewers simply avoided former slaves who were known to be hostile to whites. One scholar, Kenneth Stamp, conducted a statistical experiment on the original narratives stored in the Library of Congress. He found that slavery was remembered as a harsh institution by 7 percent of those interviewed by whites and 25 percent of those interviewed by blacks, and by 3 percent of those clearly dependent on white support but 23 percent of those who seemed to be financially independent. Stamp's research also noted a geographic effect. Thirty-eight percent of former slaves living in the North recalled slavery harshly, compared to only 16 percent of those living in the South. This suggests that the former slaves with the harshest impressions of slavery had already fled the region.

Please do not let these statistics detract from the value of the former slaves' words. The memories of these elderly men and women may have been influenced by the ghosts of the South and by the burden of old age, but they bring our history to life with a vibrancy that few historical texts can hope to possess. "Blues is a compelling, inspiring, living art," notes the great folk historian Peter Guralnick. He was writing about Tommy Johnson, Willie Brown, and Booker White, but I believe he could have just as easily been discussing Henrietta Murray, Lizzie Williams, and Isaac Potter. It is the aural quality of these narratives that I find so compelling. Without the inflections in the voices, the rhetorical asides, and the lost threads, these narratives would just be words—the dull, lifeless, brittle words too often found in historical texts. But with those qualities intact, they breathe with tone, harmony, and melody, creating an experience that is as akin to music as mere words can possibly be. I invite you now to turn the page and listen to their songs.

Prayin' to Be Set Free

James Lucas

Age approximately 105

when interviewed in Natchez, Mississippi

I was born on October 11, 1833. My young marster give me my age when he inherited the property of his uncle, Marse W. B. Withers. He was a-goin' through the papers and a-burnin' some of 'em when he found the one 'bout me. Then he says, "Jim, this'n 'bout you. It gives your birthday."

I recollect a heap 'bout slavery times, but I's all by myself now. All of my friends has left me. Even Marse Fleming has passed on. He was a little boy when I was a grown man.

I was born in a cotton field in cotton-pickin' time, and the womens fixed my mammy up so she didn't hardly lose no time at all. My mammy sho' was healthy.

Her name was Silvey, and her mammy come over to this country in a big ship. Somebody give her the name of Betty, but it warn't her right name. Folks couldn't understand a word she say. It was some sort of gibberish they called Gullah-talk, and it sound that funny. My pappy was Bill Lucas.

When I was a little chip, I used to wear coarse Lowell-cloth shirts [cheap cotton cloth. The name is derived from Lowell, Massachusetts, where it was primarily manufactured.] on the week-a-days. They was long and had big collars. When the seams ripped, the hide would show through. When I got big enough to wait 'round at the big house and go to town, I wore clean, rough clothes. The pants was white linsey-woolsey, and the shirts was rough white cotton what was wove at the plantation. In the winter, the sewin' womens made heavy clothes and knit wool socks for us. The womens wore linsey-woolsey dresses and long leggin's like the soldiers wear. This was a long, narrow wool cloth, and it wrapped round and round they legs and fasten at the top with a string.

I never went to no church, but on Sundays, a white man would preach and pray with us. And when he'd get through, us went on 'bout us own business.

At Christmas, the marster give the slaves a heap of fresh meat and whiskey for treats. But you better not get drunk. No, sir! Then on Christmas Eve, they was a big dance, and the white folks would come and see the one what dance the best. Marster and Mist'ess laugh fit to kill at the capers us cut. Then sometimes, they had big weddin's, and the young white ladies dressed the brides up like they was white. Sometimes, they sent to New Orleans for a big cake. The preacher married 'em with the same testimony [ceremony] they use now. Then everybody have a little drink and some cake. Then everybody'd get right. Us could dance near 'bout all night. The old-time fiddlers played fast music, and us all clapped hands and tromped and swayed in time to the music. Us sho' made the rafters ring.

Us slaves didn't pay no 'tention to who owned us, leastways the young ones didn't. I was raised by a marster what owned a heap of lands. Lemme see, they is called Artonish, Lockdale, and Lockleaven. They is plantations 'long the river in Wilkinson County, where I was raised. They is all 'long together.

I's sho' my first marster was Marse Jim Stamps, and his wife was Miss Lucindy. She was nice and soft goin'. Us was glad when she stayed on the plantation.

Next thing I knowed, us all belonged to Marse Withers. He was from the North, and he didn't have no wife. Marsters without wives was the devil. I knows a-plenty what I oughtn't tell to ladies. It warn't the marsters what was so mean. 'Twas them po' white-trash overseers and agents. They was mean; they was meaner than bulldogs. Wives made a big difference. They was kind and went 'bout 'mongst the slaves a-lookin' after 'em. They give out food and clothes and shoes. They doctored the little babies. When things went wrong, womens was all the time puttin' me up to tellin' the Mist'ess. Marse D. D. Withers was my young marster. He was a little man, but ever'body stepped when he came 'round.

My next marster was Pres'dent Jefferson Davis hisself. Only he warn't no pres'dent then. He was just a tall, quiet gentleman with a pretty, young wife what he married in Natchez. Her name was Miss Varina Howell, and he sho' let her have her way. I 'spect I's the only one livin' whose eyes ever seed 'em both. I talked with her when they come in the big steamboat. 'Fore us got to the big house, I told her all 'bout the goin's-on on the plantation. She was a fine lady. When I was a boy 'bout thirteen years old, they took me up the country toward Vicksburg to a place call Briarsfield. It musta been named for her old home in Natchez, what was called the Briars. I didn't belong to Marse Jeff no great while, but I ain't never forget the look of him. He was always calm like and savin' on his words. His wife was just the other way. She talked more than a-plenty.

I believes a bank sold us next to Marse L. Q. Chambers. I 'members him well. I was a house servant, and the overseer didn't hit me a lick. Marster done lay the law down. Most planters lived on they plantations just a part of the year. They would go off to Saratogy [Saratoga, New York] and places up North. Sometimes, Marse L. Q. would come down to the place with a big wagon filled with a thousand pair of shoes at one time. He had a nice wife. One day whilst I was a-waitin' on the table, I see old Marse lay his knife down just like he tired. Then he lean back in his chair, kinda still like. Then I say, "What the matter with Marse L. Q.?" Then they all jump and scream, and bless the Lord if he warn't plumb dead.

Slaves didn't know what to 'spect from freedom, but a lot of 'em hoped they would be fed and kept by the gov'ment. They all had diff'rent ways of thinkin' 'bout it. Mostly, though, they was just like me. They didn't know just exactly what it meant. It was just somethin' that the white folks and slaves all the time talk 'bout. That's all. Folks that ain't never been free don't rightly know the feel of bein' free. They don't know the meanin' of it. Slaves like us, what was owned by quality folks, was satisfied and didn't sing none of them freedom songs. I recollect one song us could sing. It went like this:

Drinkin' of the wine, drinkin' of the wine,
Oughta been in heaven three thousand years.
A-drinkin' of that wine, a-drinkin' of that wine.

I was a grown-up man with a wife and two chillun when the war broke out. You see, I stayed with the folks 'til 'long come the Yanks. They took me off and put me in the war. First, they shipped me on a gunboat. And next, they made me help dig a canal at Vicksburg. I was on the gunboat when it shelled the town. It was terrible, seein' folks a-tryin' to blow each other up. Whilst us was bull-doggin' Vicksburg in front, a Yankee army slipped in behind the Rebels and penned 'em up. I fit [fought] at Fort Pillow and Harrisburg and Pleasant Hill, and 'fore I was half through with it, I was in Baltimore and Virginny.

I was on hand when Gen'ral Lee handed his sword to Gen'ral Grant. They had him all but hemmed in, and he just nat'rally had to give up. I seen him stick his sword up in the ground.

It [the war] sho' was terrible times. These old eyes of mine seen more people crippled and dead. I's even seen 'em saw off legs with hacksaws. I tell you, it ain't right, what I seen. It ain't right at all.

Then I was buryin' Yankee soldiers. When nobody was lookin', I stripped the dead of they money. Sometimes, they had it in a belt around they bodies. Soon, I got a big old roll of foldin' money. Then I came a-trampin' back home. My folks didn't have no money but that worthless kind [Confederate money]. It was all they knowed 'bout. When I grabbed some of it and throwed it in the blazin' fire, they thought I was crazy, 'til I told 'em that ain't money, it's no 'count! Then I give my daddy a greenback and told him what it was.

After the war was over, the slaves was worse off than when they had marsters. Some of 'em was put in stockades at Angola, Loosanna [Louisiana], and some in the terrible corral at Natchez. They warn't used to the stuff the Yankees fed 'em. They caught diseases and died by the hundreds, just like flies. They had been fooled into thinkin' it would be good times, but it was the worse times they ever seen. Warn't no place for 'em to go, no bed to sleep on, and no roof over they heads. Them what could get back home set out with they minds made up to stay on the land. Most of the marsters took 'em back, so they worked the land again. I means them what lived to get back to they folks was more'n glad to work! They done had a sad lesson. Some of 'em was worse'n slaves after the war.

Them Ku Kluxes was the devil. The niggers sho' was scared of 'em, but they was more after them car- petbaggers then the niggers. I lived right in 'mongst 'em, but I wouldn't tell. I knowed 'em, but I don't talk. Sometimes, they would go right in the fields and take folks out and kill 'em. Ain't none of 'em left now. They is all dead and gone, but they sho' was rabid then. I never got in no trouble with 'em, 'cause I tended my business and kept out of they way. I'd of been killed if I'd of run 'round and done any big talkin'.

I never knowed Marse Lincoln, but I heard he was a powerful good man. I 'members plain as yesterday when he got killed and how all the flags hung at half mast. The North nearly went wild with worryin' and blamed ever'body else. Some of 'em even tried to blame the killin' on Marse Davis. I fit [fought] with the Yankees, but I thought a mighty heap of Marse Davis. He was quality.

I guess slavery was wrong, but I 'members us had some mighty good times. Some marsters was mean and hard, but I was treated good all the time. One thing I does know is that a heap of slaves was worse off after the war. They suffered 'cause they was too triflin' to work without a boss. Now, they is got to work or die. In them days, you worked and rested and knowed you'd be fed. In the middle of the day, us rested and waited for the horn to blow to go back to the field. Slaves didn't have nothin' terrible to worry 'bout if they acted right. They was mean slaves the same as they was mean marsters.

Nowadays, folks don't live right. In slav'ry time when you got sick, a white doctor was paid to get you well. Now, all you gets is some no 'count patent medicine. You is 'fraid to go to the hospital, 'cause the doctors might cut on yo' stomach. I think slavery was a lot easier than the war. That was the devil's own business. In wartimes, a man was no more than a varmint.

When my white folks told us us was free, I waited. When the soldiers come, they turned us loose like animals with nothin'. They had no business to set us free like that. They gimme 160 acres of land, but it warn't no-'count. It was in Mount Bayou, Arkansas, and was low and swampy. Warn't no land to keep lessen you lived on it. You had to clear it, drain it, and put a house on it. How I goin' drain and clear a lot of land with nothin' to do it with? Reckon somebody livin' on my land now.

I draw a federal pension now. If I lives 'til next year, I'll get $125 a month. It sho' comes in handy. I paid $800 for my house, and if I'd of thought, I'd of got one with more land. I don't want to plant nothin'. I do want to put an iron fence around it and gild it with silver paint. Then when I's gone, there it will be.

I's raised a big family. Them what ain't dead, some of 'em looks as old as I does. I got one grandchild I loves just like my own chillun. I don't rightly 'member how many chillun I had, but I ain't had but two wives. The first one died long 'bout seventeen years, and I done what the Good Book say. It say, when you goes to the graveyard to bury yo' first wife, look over the crowd and pick out the next one. That's just what I done. I picked Janie McCoy, 'cause she ain't never been married before. She's a good cook, even if she does smoke a pipe.

I sho' don't live by no rules. I just takes a little dram whenever I wants it, and I smokes a pipe 'cept when the mist'ess give me a cigar. I can't chew tobacco on 'count my teeth is gone.

Nowadays, I has a heap of misery in my knee, so I can't ride round no mo'. Durin' the war, I got a musket ball in my hip, and now that meat's all gone. It jolts around and hurts me worse. I's still right sprightly, though. I can jump that drainage ditch in front of the house, and I sho' can walk. Most every day, I walks to the little sto' on Union Street. There, I rests long enough to pass the time of day with my neighbors. My eyes is still good, but I wears glasses for show and for seein' close.

The longer I lives, the plainer I sees that it ain't right to want mo' than you can use. The Lawd put a-plenty here for ever'body. But shucks, us don't pay no mind to his teachin'. Sometimes, I gets lonesome for the friends I used to know, 'cause ain't nobody left but me. I sho' been left a fur piece behind. The white folks say, "Old Jim is the last leaf on the tree," and I 'spect they's 'bout right.

Belle Caruthers

Age 90 when interviewed
at her home in Marshall County, Mississippi

My name is Belle Garland Myers Caruthers, and I want it all put in. I was born near Wadesboro, North Carolina, in 1847. My master was Absolem Myers.

My mother was Emmaline Myers. She was brought from Virginia, and her white people had taught her to read and write. She had sixteen children.

The Myers family and slaves moved to Mississippi, but I don't remember the year. We moved in wagons, but the master and mistress came in a carriage. Colonel Myers settled near Byhalia in Marshall County. He owned a large plantation, grist mill, and a sawmill. He sawed all the lumber to build his house.

The slaves lived in the quarters. Their houses were log cabins, with stick chimneys, daubed with mud. We cooked, ate, and slept in one room, no matter how big the family. We had our own gardens, though we sometimes had to work them at night.

All cooking was done over open fireplaces. I never saw a cookstove until after the war.

I worked in the house, waited on my mistress, fanned her when she slept, and nursed the baby.

The baby had alphabet blocks to play with, and I learned my letters while she learned hers. There was a Blue Back Speller there, too. One day, the master caught me studying it, and he struck me with his muddy boot. Colonel Myers was a hard master, not kind like many of them.

I found a hymn book one day and spelled out, "When I Can Read My Title Clear." I was so happy when I saw that I could really read that I ran around telling all the other slaves. After the war, I went to Gill's School in Holly Springs. That was a school run by northern white people.

On the plantation, I played hide-and-seek, "squirrel," and games like that. Sometimes we had quiltings and suppers. We always got three days off at Christmas.

The overseer was nothing, just common white trash. If the niggers didn't get to the field by daylight, he would beat them. But he didn't put them in jail because he wanted them to work. And we worked all day Saturday.

And, my, but we were afraid of the patterollers. They marched about the country, and whenever they found a nigger belonging to one man on another man's plantation, they punished him hard.

One day during the war, a Yankee officer named Major Berg sat on the front porch and talked to old Miss. She told him she had six sons in the Southern army and wished she had sixty to give. He said he admired her patriotism.

Then she told him if he would have her house guarded she would cook him the best meal he ever ate. And he did, and she had a grand dinner cooked and served him in style. On account of that, our house was not burned when all the others in the neighborhood were.

One day when I was bringing in some wood, I caught sight of the jars of gold and silver old Miss had hid under some bricks. I told her and nobody else, not even my mother, and she moved them to a safer place.

One day in '65, young master came home. I knew when I heard his footsteps on the porch that he was awful downcast. The war was over, but we didn't know it 'til he came home.

He came to his mother's room, and I met him at the door. He said, "Belle, where is Ma?" And I said, "She died one week ago today." He just turned away without a word and walked the floor all night.

The Negroes never heard of Lincoln 'til after the

war, but if the white people had listened to him and freed their slaves there wouldn't have been a war. But he was assassinated. If you will notice, all the presidents that have been assassinated were Republicans.

I joined the Methodist Church in 1867 and have been a church worker ever since. I taught in Sunday school for thirty years.

In '68, I married Caruthers. Captain Myers was clerk in the courthouse and wouldn't let us have a license, so we went to Oxford and married there.

I taught at the Negro school here in Holly Springs until my daughter graduated in '91. Then I thought it was time to quit.

I have been writing the Negro section of the county paper, *The South-Reporter*, now for the past ten years and guess I'll keep it up as long as I can see to write.

One time, President Theodore Roosevelt was in Memphis, and I was there to hear him speak. I was mighty proud when my son went up, and the president shook hands with him.

I have lived to see many changes, but there is one thing I've noticed and can't understand—the elements are not as thick with stars as they used to be!

Some colored people say slavery was better because they had no responsibility. It is true, they were fed, clothed, and sheltered, but I'm like the man that said, "Give me freedom or give me death!"

Prince Johnson_____

Age approximately 90
when interviewed in Coahoma County, Mississippi

My grandfather Peter, Grandmother Millie, my father, John, and my mother, Frances, all came from Alabama to Yazoo County, Mississippi, to live in the Love family. Their names were Dennis when they came, but after the custom of them days, they took the name of Love from their new owner. Me and all of my brothers and sisters were born right there. There were eleven head of us. I was the oldest. Then came Harry, John, William, Henry, Phyllis, Polly, Nellie, Virginia, Millia, and the baby Ella. We all lived in the quarters, and our beds were homemade. They had wooden legs and canvas stretched across. I can't remember so much about the quarters because about that time the young Miss married Colonel Johnson and moved to his place in Carroll County. She carried with her over one hundred head of darkies, and our names was changed from Love to Johnson. My new master was sure a fine gentleman. He lived in a big white house that had two stories on it and big white posts in front. There were flowers all around it that just set it off.

Master took me for the houseboy, and I carried my head high. He would say to me, "Prince, do you know who you were named for?" I would say to him, "Yes sir, Prince Albert." And then he would say to me, "Well, always carry yourself like he did." To this day, I holds myself like Master said.

On certain days of the week one of the old men on the place took us house servants to the field to learn us to work. We was brought up to know how to do anything that came to hand. At odd times, Master would let us work for outsiders, and we could use the money we made for anything we pleased. My grandmother sold enough corn to buy her two feather beds. We always had plenty to eat. The old folks did the cooking for all the field hands, 'cept on Sunday when each family cooked for theyself. Old Miss would come every Sunday morning with sugar and white flour. We would most generally have fish, rabbits, possums, or coons. Lord, those possums was good eating. I can taste them now. Folks these days don't know nothing about good eating. My master had a great big garden for ever'body, and I ain't never seen such sweet 'tatoes as grew in that garden. They were so sweet the sugar would bust right through the peeling when you roast them on the hearth.

Old Aunt Emily cooked for all the children on the place. Half an hour by the sun, they were all called in to supper. They had pot likker and ash cake and such things as would make them grow to be strong and healthy. Those children didn't know nothing about all those fancy ailments what children have now. They ran and played all day in their shirttails in the summertime, but when winter came they had good warm clothes same as us older ones. One day, Master's children and all the colored children slipped off to the orchard. They were eating green apples as fast as they could swallow, when who should come riding up but Master himself. He lined them all up, black and white alike, and cut a keen switch. There was not a one in that line that didn't get a few licks. Then he called the old doctor woman and made her give them every one a dose of medicine. There wasn't one of them that got sick.

Master and old Miss had five children. They are all dead and gone now, and I am still here. One of his sons was a Supreme Judge before he died. My folks were sure quality. Master bought all the little places around us so he wouldn't have no poor white-trash neighbors. He owned about 3,500 acres and at least 150 slaves. Every morning about four o'clock, we could hear that horn blow for us to get up and go to the field. We always quit work before the sun went down and never worked at night.

The overseer was a white man. His name was Josh Neighbors, but the driver was a colored man, "Old Man Henry." He wasn't allowed to mistreat nobody. The rule was if a nigger wouldn't work, he would be sold. Another rule on that place was that if a man got dissatisfied he was to go to old Master and ask him to put him in his pocket. That meant he wanted to be sold, and the money he brought would be put in the pocket. I ain't never known of but two asking to be put in the pocket, and both of them was put in.

They had jails in those days, but they were built for white folk. No colored person was ever put in one of them 'til afer the war. We didn't know nothing about them things. Course old Miss knowed about them 'cause she knowed everything. I recollect she told me one day that she had learning in five different languages. None of us didn't have no learning at all. That is, we didn't have no book learning. There wasn't no teachers or anything of that kind, but we sure were taught to be Christians. Everything on that place was a bluestocking Presbyterian. When Sunday came, we dressed all clean and nice and went to church. There wasn't no separate church for the colored. We went to the white folks' church and set in the gallery. We had a fine preacher. His name was Cober. He could sure give out the words of wisdom. We didn't have the baptizing like was had on heaps of the places, 'cause Presbyterians don't go down under the water like the Baptists does.

Old Miss wouldn't stand for no such things as voodoo and haints. When she inspected us once a week, you better not have no charm 'round your neck. She would not as much as let us wear a bag of asafetida, and most folks believed that would keep off sickness. She called such as that superstition. She says we was enlightened Christian Presbyterians, and as such we must conduct ourselves. She didn't want to hear of no stories being told 'bout haints and ghosts 'cause there wasn't no such things. I 'spect she was right 'cause I ain't never seed one in all the ninety years I've been living.

If one of the slaves died, he was sure given a grand Christian funeral. All of us mourners were there. Services were conducted by the white preacher. Just before the war came on, my master called me to him and told me he was going to take me to North Carolina to his brother for safekeeping. Right then I knowed something was wrong, and I was wishing from the bottom of my heart the 'Publicans would stay out of our business and not get us all 'sturbed in the mind.

Nobody worked after dinner on Saturday. We took that time to scrub ourselves and our houses, so as to be ready for inspection Sunday morning. Some Saturday nights we had dances. The same old fiddler played for us that played for the white folks. And could he play!

When he got that old fiddle out, you couldn't keep your foots still. When Christmas came, that was the time of all times on that old plantation. They don't have such as that now. Every child brought a stocking up to the big house to be filled. They all wanted one of old Miss's stockings 'cause now she weighed near on to three hundred pounds. Candy was put in piles for each person. When their names were called, they walked up and got it. We didn't work on New Year's Day. We could go to town or anywhere we liked, but we didn't have no kind of celebration.

The most fun a person can have is at a corn shucking. You have two captains, and they each choose the ones they want on their side. Then the shucking begins. The last one I 'tended, the side I was on beat by three barrels. We put our captain on our shoulders and rode him up and down while everybody cheered and clapped their hands like the world was coming to an end. You can't make mention of nothing good that we didn't have to eat after the shucking.

I studies about those days now. The big parties at the white folks' house, and me all dressed up with tallow on my face to make it shine, serving the guests. Just when everything was going fine, a sad thing happened. A thing I ain't never made mention of before. My young mistress, Miss Farrell, the one named for her ma, ups and runs off and marries the son of the Irish ditcher that dug all the ditches on the place. My miss wouldn't have done that if they had let her married the man she wanted to. They didn't think he was good enough for her, so just to spite them, she marries the son of the Irish ditcher. Old Miss wouldn't have nothing more to do with her, same as if she wasn't her own child, but I would go over to see her and carry her milk and things out of the garden. It was pitiful to see my miss poor. When I couldn't stand it no longer, I walks right up to old Miss and I says, "Old Miss, does you know Miss Farrell ain't got no cow?" She just set there like she ain't heard me and put her lips together tight as she could, but she won't say nothing, so I couldn't do no more but walk off and leave her. Pretty soon she called, "Prince!" I says, "Yes, ma'am." She says, "Seeing you is so concerned 'bout Miss Farrell not having no cow you better take one to her." I says, "Where is the rope?" And she says, "I don't know nothing 'bout no rope." I found the rope and carried the best cow and calf in the lot to Miss Farrell. Shortly after that, I left with old Master to go to North Carolina.

Things went on on his brother's place pretty much as they did at home. I stayed there all four years of the war and longer. I couldn't leave because the menfolks all went to war, and I had to stay and protect the womenfolks. The day peace was declared, wagonloads of people rode all through the place telling us we was free and that we didn't have no more miss or master. The old colonel was killed in battle, and his wife had died.

The young master called us in and said it was all true, that we were as free as he was, and we could leave whenever we got ready. He said his money wasn't good any more, and he didn't have no other money to pay us with. I can't recollect whether he got new money and paid us or not, but I do 'member we every last one of us stayed.

I never left that place 'til my young master, Mr. Jim Johnson, the one that was the Supreme Judge, came for me. He was living then in South Carolina. He took us all home with him. We got there in time to vote for Governor Wade Hamilton. We put him in office, too. [Editor's note: This reference is probably to Wade Hampton, who was a Confederate general and served as governor of South Carolina from 1877-79. Johnson may be referring to Hampton's first bid for governor, which he lost in 1865, although Johnson is mistaken about the outcome.]

I've seen many a patrol in my lifetime, but they never did have enough nerve to come on us's place. Now the Ku Klux was different. I have ridden with them many a time. It was the only way in them days to keep order. When I was about twenty-two years old, I married Clara Breaden. I had two children by her, Diana and Davis. My second wife's name was Annie Beth Woods. I had six children by her—Mary, Ella, John D., Claud, William, and Prince, Jr. Three boys and two girls are still living. I live with my daughter Claud, who is farming a place about five miles from Clarksdale. I have about fifteen head of grandchildren, and every last one of them is farmers.

Things is all peaceful now, but the world was sure stirred up when Abraham Lincoln was elected. I remember well when they killed him. We had a song about him that went like this:

> Jefferson Davis rode the milk-white steed,
> Lincoln rode the mule.
> Jeff Davis was a mighty fine man,
> And Lincoln was a fool.

When things all got peaceful-like, I begun yearning to get back to my old home in Mississippi. So I came, and I been here ever since. When I got back to Mississippi, I went in with a man named Mr. Jim Somerville. The first thing I done was to join the Democrat Club at Carrollton. I joined that club, put on the red shirt, and hoped [helped] them run all of the scalawags away from there. My young master had always told me to live for my country. I had seed too much of that war not to know all about what was going on.

After everything got quiet and peaceful-like in Mississippi, I started farming on Mr. Armstrong's place. He was a big rich man what lived near Vaiden. He sure treated the folks on his place fair and square. I bought 360 acres of land from him. I is a nigger what has sure been prosperous in my life. Besides the land I had, I owned thirty head of cattle, fourteen mules, and sixty hogs. Every year, I was making 125 bales of cotton. I was bringing up my family right, teaching my children to be good bluestocking Presbyterians. For thirty years, I stayed right there, always making a good living. All around the country I was knowed, and everybody had confidence in me.

I expected to spend the rest of my days right there on the same place, but you never can tell in this life what's going to happen. During the Cleveland administration, cotton went to a nickle a pound. That was the year I lost my land. Mr. Armstrong went broke, and I went right down with him. We was both plumb busted.

I crossed over the creek and bought me a place for $1,500, trying to see if I couldn't get on my feet again. That man I bought from sure did treat me bad. My young master came to see 'bout me, and he told me there wasn't no use my paying no more on that place 'cause they ain't never made me out no bond for title. No matter how much I paid it wouldn't do no good without the bond for title. Any man that would do the like of that can't 'spect their children to come to no good. I left that place and went to the Dike plantation near Drew. I was anxious to get to the Delta 'cause the boll weevil was getting bad where I was. I made two crops there in the year 1922-23. They treated me bad there, too. I made 76 bales of cotton and didn't get my seed money. From there, we went from place to place, working as sharecroppers. Things was so bad during the Depression it was hard to make a living anywhere. Four or five years ago, we moved on this place with Mr. Mays, and we is getting on tolerable well here. My crop is good, and I's got a nice garden.

Maybe things is better as they is today. Most folks say so anyway, but if old Master was living, I for one would be better off. I can hear him say to me now, "Prince Albert, who is you named for? Well then, hold your head high so folks can see you is aristocratic."

Calline Brown

Age unknown when interviewed
at her home in Coahoma County, Mississippi

My mind ain't sprightly like it used to be, and heaps of things what went on when I was young I forgets, and heaps of them what I want to forget I can't. Them was terrible days. My master and miss was the meanest folks what ever lived. They warn't nothing but poor-white trash what had never had nothing in their lives. Missus's sister was poor-white trash, too, but her and her husband had got a little prosperous raising cotton and bought a few slaves. Their name was Howard. You know how some folks is when they gets up a little in the world. They wants to see their family pull out of the mire. So Mrs. Howard gave her sister, Mrs. Mullens, a little place back in the woods, and my mammy and daddy and us children. We had to clear it up and work it. There warn't nothing on that place. Not a cow, not a hog, nothing— not even so much as a feather from a chicken. They ain't got no money to buy us no clothes or shoes, so we goes in rags, and barefooted, even in the winter. Many is the time I have helped pull pine logs out of water, ankle deep and coated with ice, me in my bare feet.

It sure was pitiful the way things went them days. We didn't know much about what was going on in the outside world. The little town nearest us was called Rock Port. It is in Copiah County. It was seldom we left the place. We worked from daylight to dark, but there warn't no such thing as satisfying either Master or Missus. We never knew when we were going to be whipped. Even after Master got so crippled he couldn't walk, he would call us to him and strike us with his crutch. I don't know nothing 'bout no dates. Figures goes right out of my head. But I knows we stayed there a long, long time. I remember well when the stars fell. They didn't come straight down like most folks thinks they did. They went right on slanting-like towards the North, and they looked like balls of fire. We was all so scared we screamed and cried and prayed all at the same time. It sure looked like the end of the world had come, and I 'spect we would have been all burned to death if the good Lord hadn't let them stars go slanting-like to the North.

We didn't even know the war was over. The white

folks tried to keep it out of the ears about freedom. Some of the Yankees must have told my daddy about it. He ain't made no mention to nobody 'bout what he heared, and that very night he disappears. He was gone a long time. It must have been nigh on a week. We was all asleep in the middle of the night when he came slipping in. My mammy was in bed with a young baby. He called us all and said to get our things together. He was going to take us away across the river. We didn't have no things to get 'cept a few rags, and they were mostly used to put around the baby. The boat he was to take us in was so little he could only take one or two at a time. But we all made it over before daylight caught us.

There was a house all ready for us on Mr. John Potter's place. He had a good wife named Miss Malinda. She sure was good to us. She got us clothes and shoes and even so much as gave us a cow. Our trouble would have been all over, if it hadn't been for that Ku Klux. Lord have mercy, how they did scare us! They had a song they sang to you that they would be back to see you. I did know the words to that song, but it has skipped my mind since I have gotten so old. When they came, they fought, beat, and sometime killed. Glory be to God, they never came nigh my house! I stayed on that place many a long day and raised a big family of children. Most of them is dead now, so I came to the Delta to live with my daughter, Mary. She cared for me mighty good 'til her husband died. Since that time she does the best she can to support us by picking cotton, and the like of such. We lives here all alone and heaps of time we talk about the long ago. The other night she said to me, "How come you reckon the Ku Klux didn't come to your house?" I says, "I just don't know, but I am mighty thankful I never failed to put salt on the fire every time I heared them old squeench owls."

Charlie Davenport

Age approximately 100 when interviewed
at his home in Adams County, Mississippi

I is named Charlie Davenport and 'cordin' to the way I figgers, I ought to be nearly a hundred. Nobody knows my birthday 'cause all my white folks is gone. I was born one night, and the very next mornin' my poor little mammy died. Her name was Lucindy. My pa was William Davenport. When I was a little mite, they turned me over to the "granny nurse" on the plantation what tended to the picanninnies [small children]. She got a woman who had a young baby to nurse me, so I didn't know no difference. Any woman what had a baby 'bout my age would wet-nurse me, so I growed up in the quarters and was as well and happy as any other chile.

When I could tote 'taters, they let me pick 'em up in the field. Us always hid a pile away what us roasted in the ashes at night.

Ole Mammy nearly always made a heap of dewberry and simmon [persimmon] wine. And us little tykes would gather black walnuts in the woods and store 'em under the cabins to dry. At night when the work was all done and the candles out, we'd set around the dyin' embers and eat a pan of cracked walnuts, pickin' the meat out with horseshoe nails. Then Mammy would pour herself and her old man a cup of wine. We never got to taste it lessen us got sick. Then she'd mess it up with wild-cherry bark and say "drink that down." It nearly strangled us, but us gulped it down.

Aventine, where I was born and bred, was across Second Creek. It was a big plantation with 'bout a hundred head of people livin' there. It was only one of Marster's places 'cause he was one of the richest and highest quality gentlemen in the whole country. I's telling you the truth, us didn't belong to no white trash. Our marster was the Honorable Mister Gabriel Shields hisself. Everybody knows 'bout him. He married a Surget. Them Surgets was pretty devilish, for they was the richest family in the land. They was the out-fightin'ist, out-cussin'est, fastest ridin', hardest drinkin', out-spendin'est folks I ever seen. But Lord, Lord, they was gentlemen. The ladies was beautiful, with big black eyes and soft white hands, but they was high-strung, too.

Our marster had a town mansion what's pictured in a lot of books. It was called "Montebella," and the big columns still stands yet at the end of Shields Lane. It burned 'bout thirty years ago.

I is part Injun. Can't you see I ain't got no nigger nose, and my hair is so long I has to keep it wrapped? I is often heard my mammy was reddish-lookin' with long, straight black hair. Her pa was a full-blooded Choctaw. Young as she was, I been told that nobody dare meddle with her. She didn't do much talkin' but she sho' was a good worker. My pappy had Injun blood, too, but his hair was kinky.

The Choctaws lived all 'round Second Creek. Some of them had cabins, like settled folks. I can remember their last chief. He was a tall, powerful-built man named "Big Sam." What he said was the law, 'cause he was the boss of the whole tribe. One rainy night, he was killed in a saloon down in "Natchez Under the Hill." The Injuns went wild with rage and grief. They sung and wailed and did a heap o' low mutterin'. The sheriff kept a steady watch on 'em, 'cause he was feared they would do somethin' rash. After a long while, he kinda let up in his vigilance. Then, some of the Choctaw men slipped in town and stabbed the man what they believed killed Big Sam. I 'member it well.

I growed up in the quarters. Our houses was clean and snug. We was better fed then I is now, and warmer, too, 'cause us had blankets and quilts filled with home-raised wool. I just loved layin' in the big, fat feather bed, a-hearin' the rain patter on the roof.

All the little darkies helped bring in wood, and us swept the yard with brush brooms. Sometimes us played together in the street, which run the length of the quarters. Us throwed horseshoes, jumped poles, walked on stilts, and played marbles. Sometimes us made bows and arrows, too, and we learned to shoot like little Injuns.

A heap of times our ole granny would brush our hide with a peach-tree limb. But us needed it 'cause us stole eggs and roasted them. She sho' wouldn't stand for no stealin' if she know it.

We wore Lowell-cloth shirts. It was a coarse tow sacking. In winter we had linsey-woolsey pants and heavy cowhide shoes. They was made in three sizes, big, little, and medium. They wasn't no right or left, but sorta club-shaped, so us could wear 'em on either foot.

I was a teasin', mischievous chile, and the overseer's little girl got it in for me. He was a big, hard-fisted Dutchman bent on gettin' riches. So he trained his pasty-faced chile to tattle on us. She got a heap of people whipped. I knowed it, but I was hasty. One day she hit me with a stick, and I throwed it back at her. Just then, up walked her pa. He seen what I done, but he didn't see her. It wouldn't of made no difference if he had.

He snatched me in the air and toted me to a stump and laid me across it. I didn't have but one thickness between me and daylight. Gentlemen, but he laid it on me with that stick! I thought I'd die, and all the time his mean little girl was gloatin' in my misery. I yelled and prayed to the Lord 'til he quit. Then he say to me: "From now on you works in the field. I ain't goin' to have no vicious boy like you around my womenfolk."

I was too little for fieldwork, but next mornin' I went to choppin' cotton. After that, I was made a regular field hand. When I growed up, I was a ploughman and could sho' lay off a pretty cotton row.

On Sunday us rested and had meetin' in a log house, where a white preacher told us 'bout the way to salvation.

When I was a little boy, they was a slave uprisin' planned. It was before the war broke out. The slaves had it all worked out how they was goin' to march on Natchez after slayin' all their white folks. Us folks wouldn't join 'em, 'cause what we want to kill ole Marse for? One night, a strange nigger come in, and he harangued the ole folks, but they wouldn't budge. While he was talking, up ride the sheriff and a passel of men. He was a powerful big black feller named Jupiter, and when he see who was comin', he turned and fled in a cornfield.

My granny told me next day that they caught him hidin' in a bayou and hung him on a limb. They didn't need no trial 'cause he was caught rilin' the folks to murder.

I reckon I was 'bout fifteen when honest Abe Lincoln, what called hisself a railsplitter, come here to talk with us. He went all through the country just a rantin' and preachin' 'bout us bein' his black brothers. Ole Marse didn't know nothin' 'bout it 'cause it was sorta secret-like. It sho' riled the niggers up, and lots of 'em run away. I sho' heard him but didn't pay him no mind. [Editor's Note: Davenport may be inaccurately remembering a visit from John Brown or his emissary, an event reported in the *Vicksburg Whig* after Brown was executed.] When the war broke out, our ole Dutch overseer went back north. We was powerful glad and hoped he'd get his neck broke.

After that the Yankees came swoopin' down on us. My own pappy took off with 'em. He joined a company what fought at Vicksburg. Them Yankees sho' made my daddy work. They put a pick in his hand instead of a gun and made him dig a big ditch in front of Vicksburg. I was plenty big enough to fight but didn't hanker to tote no gun. I stayed on the plantation and put in a crop. It was powerful uneasy times after that, but what I care 'bout freedom?

By that time I was stayin' on Fish Pond plantation, closer to town. Then 'long came the white folks tellin' us we must burn all the cotton so the enemy can't get it.

We piled it high in the fields like great mountains. It made my innards hurt to see fire touched to somethin' that had cost us niggers so much labor and honest sweat. If I coulda hid some of it in the bayou I would, but the boss searched everywhere.

The little niggers thought it was fun. They laughed and brung out big armfuls from the cotton house. One little black girl clapped her hands and jumped in a big heap. Then the wind pick up the flame and spread it like lightnin'. It spread so fast that 'fore we could bat our eyes, she was in a mountain of fire. She come up all covered with flames and screamin', "Lord help me!" Us snatched her up and rolled her on the ground, but she died in a few minutes.

Our ole marster's sons went to war. The one what us loved the best never come home no more. Us mourned him plenty 'cause he was so jolly and happy-like and free with his change. Us all felt cheered when he come around.

Personally, I believe in what Mr. Davis done. He done the only thing a gentlemen could do. He told Mr. Abe Lincoln to tend to his own business, and he'd tend to his own. But Lincoln was a fightin' man, and he come down here to other folks' plantations. That made Mr. Davis so all-fired mad that he spit hard between his teeth and say: "I'll whip the socks off them damn Yankees."

That's how it all come about. My white folks lost money, cattle, slaves, and cotton, but they was still better off than most folks. I stayed with 'em, but they is most all gone now. I believes they would look after me now if they knowed I was on charity.

Like all the fool niggers of that time, I was right smartly bit by the freedom bug for a while. It sounded powerful nice to be told: "You don't have to chop cotton no more. You can throw that hoe down and go fishin' whensoever the notion strike you. And you can roam around at night and court gals just as late as you please. Ain't no marster going to say you is got to be back when the clock strikes nine."

I was fool enough to believe all that kind of stuff. But to tell the honest truth to God, most of us didn't know ourselves was no better off. Freedom meant we could leave where we'd been born and bred, but it also meant we had to scratch for ourselves. Them what left the ole plantation seemed so all-fired glad to get back that I made my mind up to stay put.

My white folks talked plain to me. They said real sad-like: "Charlie, you is been a dependence, but now you can go if you is so desirous. But if you wants to stay with us, you can sharecrop. There is a house for you, and wood to keep you warm, and a mule to work. We ain't got much cash, but we is got land, and you can always count on havin' plenty of vittles. Do just as you please." When I looked at my marse and knowed he needed me, I's pleased to stay. My marster never forced me to do nary thing.

I knows a-plenty 'bout the Ku Kluxes. They was sho' 'nough devils walkin' the earth seekin' what they could devour. They larruped [whipped] the hide off all the uppity niggers and drive the white trash back where they belonged.

Us niggers didn't have no secret meetin's. All us had was church meetin's in arbors out in the woods. The preachers would exhort us that we was the chillun of Israel in the wilderness, and the Lord done sent us to take that land of milk and honey. But how us going to take land what was already took?

A heap of niggers voted for a little while. Us had a nigger sheriff named Winston. He was a gingercake color and powerful mean when he got riled. There was several black men what held office. The chief one was named Lynch, and he cut a big figure up in Washington. In them days, nobody but niggers and shawl-strop folks [carpetbaggers] voted. My old marse didn't vote, and if anybody knowed what was what, he did. Sense didn't count in them days. It was powerful ticklish times, and I left votin' alone. Sheriff Winston was a slave, and if my memory ain't failed me, so was Lynch.

The shawl-strop folks what come in to take over the country told us we had a right to go to all the balls, church meetin's, and entertainment the white folks give. But one night a bunch of uppity niggers went to an entertainment in Memorial Hall. They dressed theyselves fit to kill and walked down the aisle and took seats in the very front. But just as they got good and set down, the curtain dropped and all the white folks rise up without sayin' a word. They marched out the buildin' with their chins up, and them niggers was left settin' in a empty hall.

That's the way it happened every time a nigger tried to get too uppity. That night after the breakin' up of that entertainment, the Ku Kluxes rid through the land. I heard they grabbed every nigger what walked right down that aisle, but ain't heard yet what they done with 'em.

Dora Franks

Age unknown

when interviewed in Aberdeen, Mississippi

I was born in Choctaw County, but I never knowed exactly how old I was, 'cause none of my folks could read and write. I reckon I's 'bout a hundred, 'cause I was a big girl long time befo' Surrender. I was old enough to marry two years after that.

My mammy come from Virginny. Her name was Harriet Brewer. My daddy was my young marster. His name was Marster George Brewer, and my mammy always told me that I was his. I know that there was some difference 'tween me and the rest of her chillun, 'cause they was all coal black, and I was even lighter than I is now. Lord, it's been to my sorrow many a time, 'cause the chillun used to chase me 'round and holler at me, "Old yellow nigger." They didn't treat me good, neither.

I stayed in the house most of the time with Miss Emmaline. I loved her 'cause she was so good to me. She taught me how to weave and spin. 'Fore I was bigger'n a minute I could do things that lots of the old hands couldn't come nigh doin'. She and Marse Bill had 'bout eight chillun, but most of 'em was grown when I come 'long. They was all mighty good to me and wouldn't 'low nobody to hurt me.

I 'members one time when they all went off and left me with a old black woman call Aunt Caroline what done the cookin' 'round the place some of the time. When they left the house, I went in the kitchen and asked her for a piece of white bread like the white folk eat. She haul off and slap me down and call me all kind of names that I didn't know what they meant. My nose bled and ruined the nice, clean white dress I had on. When Mist'ess come back Marse George was with her. She asked me what on earth happen to me, and I told her. They call Caroline in the room and asked her if what I say were the truth. She tell 'em it was, and they sent her away. I hear tell that they whip her so hard that she couldn't walk no mo'.

Us never had no big funerals or weddin's on the place. Didn't have no marryin' of any kind. Folks in them days just sorter hitched up together and call theyselves man and wife. All the colored folks was buried on what they call Platnum Hill. They didn't have no markers nor nothin' at the graves. They was just sunk-in places. My brother Frank showed me once where my mammy was buried. Us didn't have no preachin', or singin', or nothin', neither. Us didn't even get to have meetin's on Sunday 'less us slip off and go to some other plantation. Course, I got to go with the white folks some-times and set in the back or on the steps. That was when I was little.

Lots of niggers would slip off from one plantation to the other to see some other niggers. They would al-ways manage to get back 'fore daybreak. The worse thing I ever heard 'bout was once when my Uncle Alf run off to "jump the broom." That was what they called goin' to see a woman. He didn't come back by daylight, so they put the nigger hounds after him. They smelled his trail down in the swamp and found where he was hidin'.

Now, he was one of the biggest niggers on the place and a powerful-fast worker. But they took and give him 100 lashes with the cat of ninety-nine tails. His back was somethin' awful, but they put him in the field to work while the blood was still a-runnin'. He work right hard 'til they left. Then, when he got up to the end of the row next to the swamp, he lit out again.

They never found him that time. They say he found a cave and fix him up a room where he could live. At nights he would come out on the place and steal enough to eat and cook it in his little dugout. When the war was over, and the slaves was freed, he come out. When I saw him, he look like a hairy ape, without no clothes on and hair growin' all over his body.

My marster had a whole passel of niggers on his place. When any of 'em would get sick, they would go to the wood and get herbs and roots and make tea for 'em to drink. Hogweed and May apples was the best things I knowed of. Sometimes old Mist'ess doctored 'em herself. One time a bunch of us chillun was playin' in the woods and found some of them May apples. Us ate a lot of 'em and got awful sick. They dosed us up on grease and Samson snake root to clean us out. And it sho' done a good job. I's been a-usin' that snake root ever since.

The first thing that I 'member hearin' 'bout the war was one day when Marse George come in the house and tell Miss Emmaline that they's goin' to have a bloody war. He say he feared all the slaves would be took away. She say if that was true she feel like jumpin' in the well. I hate to hear her say that, but from that minute I started prayin' for freedom. All the rest of the women done the same.

The war started pretty soon after that, and all the menfolks went off and left the plantation for the woman and the niggers to run. Us seen the soldiers pass by most ever'day. Once the Yankees come and stole a lot of the hosses and somethin' to eat. They even took the trunkful of 'Federate [Confederate] money that was hid in the swamp. How they found that us never knowed.

Marse George come home 'bout two years after the war started and married Miss Martha Ann. They had always been sweethearts. They was promised 'fore he left.

Marse Lincoln and Marse Jeff Davis is two I 'members 'bout. But, Lord, that was a long time back! Us liked Marse Jeff Davis the best on the place. Us even made up a song 'bout him, but I can't even 'member the first line of that song. You see, when I got 'ligion, I asked the Lord to take all the other songs out of my head and make room for his word.

Since then it's the hardest thing in the world for me to 'member the songs us used to dance by. I do 'member a few like "Shoe, Fly," "Old Dan Tucker," and "Run, Nigger, Run, the Patteroller Catch You." I don't 'member much of the words. I does 'member a little of "Old Dan Tucker." It went this way:

> Old Dan Tucker was a mighty mean man,
> He beat his wife with a fryin' pan.
> She hollered and she cried, "I's goin' to go,
> They's plenty of men, won't beat me so.
>
> Get out of the way, Old Dan Tucker,
> You come too late to get yo' supper.
>
> Old Dan Tucker, he got drunk,
> Fell in the fire, kicked up a chunk,
> Red-hot coal got down his shoe.
> Oh, Great Lord, how the ashes flew.

Get out of the way, Old Dan Tucker,
You come too late to get yo' supper.

When the war was over, my brother Frank slipped in the house where I was still stayin'. He tol' me us was free and for me to come out with the rest. 'Fore sundown there warn't one nigger left on the place. I hear tell later that the mist'ess and the gals had to get out and work in the fields to help gather in the crop.

Frank found us a place to work and put us all in the field. I never worked in the field before. I'd faint away most ever'day 'bout eleven o'clock. It was the heat. Some of 'em would have to tote me to the house. I'd soon come to. Then I had to go back to the field. Us was on Marse Davis Cox's place then.

Two years later, I met Pet Franks and us married. The Coxes was good folks and give us a big weddin'. All the white folks and the niggers for miles around come to see us get married. The niggers had a big supper and had a peck to eat. Me and Pet ain't been a-livin' together for the last twenty-three years. Us just couldn't get 'long together, so us quit. He lives out at Acker's Fishing Lodge now and does the cookin' for 'em.

I never will forget the Klu Klux Klan. Never will I forget the way that horn sound at night when they was a-goin' after some mean nigger. Us'd all run and hide. Us was livin' on the Troup place then, near old Hamilton, in one o' the brick houses back of the house where they used to keep the slaves. Marse Alec Troup was one of the Klu Kluxes, and so was Marse Thad Willis that lived close by. They'd make plans together sometime and I'd hear 'em. One time they caught me listenin', but they didn't do nothin' to me, 'cause they knowed I warn't going to tell.

Young folks today is going straight to the devil. All they do all day and all night is run 'round and drink corn likker and ride in automobiles. I's got a granddaughter here, and she's that wild. I worries a right smart 'bout her, but it don't do no good, 'cause her mammy let her do just like she pleases anyhow.

I tells you the one thing I worries 'bout most. That is the white folks what lives here 'mongst the niggers. You know what kinda folks they is, and it sho' is a bad influence. You know niggers ain't supposed to always know the right from the wrong. They ain't got marsters to teach 'em now. For the white folks to come down here and do like they do, I tells you, it ain't right. The quality white folks oughta do somethin' 'bout it.

I's had a hard life, but I puts my faith in the Lord and I know ever'thing going to come out all right. I's lived a long life and will soon be a hundred, I guess. I's glad that slavery is over, 'cause the Bible don't say nothin' 'bout it bein' right. I's a good Christian. I get sorta restless most of the time and has to keep busy to keep from thinkin' too much.

Della Buckley

Age unknown when interviewed
at her home in Meridian, Mississippi

I ain't never studied 'bout how old I is; that's somethin' I ain't never paid any 'tention to. I was borned in Montgomery on the Eastley plantation, kinda out in the country. The lady I nuss'd [nursed] for was all time travelin' back and forth to Meridian to see her husband. He worked there. Finally she come on to Meridian for good, and I come with her.

When I was 'bout grown, I started cookin', but I learned to cook good befo' I started workin' for Boss Williams and ole Miss. I 'spect I was 'bout thirty-five then. I married right here in my own house in they backyard; married Pretty. That's what they calls him, 'cause he's so ugly, I reckon. I had fo' chillun, but they all dead.

They do say I cooks right good; musta been cookin' for 'em might' nigh forty years. They all time havin' comp'ny. When Boss's gent'men friends comes from New York and Baltimore, they brags right smart on my spoonbread and such. But they ain't but one sho' 'nough way to cook a possum. I'll tell you just how I does it.

First you gets the boy to clean him for you; scrape him 'til he get white. Then you soaks him all night in salten water. Take him out in the mornin' and drain him and wipe him off nice and dry. Then you par-boils him a while. Then you takes him out and grease him all over with butter and rub flour all over him and rub pepper in with it. Then you baste him with some of the juice what you par-boiled him in. Then you puts him in the stove and lets him bake. Ever' time you opens the stove do' [door], you baste him with his gravy. Peel yo' sweet pertaters and bake along with him 'til they is nice and soft and brown like the possum hisself. Sprinkle in flour to thicken yo' gravy just like you was makin' reg'lar chicken gravy. When he's nice and brown, you puts a pertater in his mouth and one on each side, and yo' possum is ready to eat.

Sam McAllum

Age 95 when interviewed
in his home at Meridian, Mississippi

The first town I ever seen were DeKalb in Kemper County. The Stephenson plantation where I were born warn't but 'bout thirteen miles north of DeKalb. I was born the second of September in 1842. My mammy belonged to the Stephensons, and my pappy belonged to Marster Lewis Barnes. His plantation warn't so very far from Stephensons'. The Stephensons and Barneses were kin white people. My pappy were a old man when I were born—I were the baby child. After he died, my mammy marry a McAllum nigger.

They were 'bout thirty slaves at Stephensons'. My mammy worked in the field, and her mammy, Lillie, were the yard woman. She looked after the little colored chillun.

I don't recollect any playthings us had 'cept a ball my young marster gimme. He were Sam Lewis Stephenson, 'bout my age. The little colored chillun would play "Blind Man Hidin'," and just whatever come to hand.

My young marster learned me out of his speller, but Mist'ess whupped me. She say I didn't need to learn nothin' 'cept how to count so's I could feed the mules without colickin' 'em. You give 'em ten ears of corn to the mule. If you give 'em more, it would colick 'em, and they'd die. They cost more'n a nigger would. That were the first whuppin' I ever got—when me and my young marster were a-spellin'.

I stayed with him special, but I waited on all the white folks' chillun at the Stephensons'. I carried the foot tub in at night and washed they foots, and I'd pull the trundle bed out from under the other bed. All boys slept in the same room.

Then I were a yard boy and waited on the young marster and mist'ess. Hadn't been to the field then— hadn't worked yet.

Mr. Stephenson were a surveyor, and he fell out with Mr. McCallum and had a lawsuit. He had to pay it in darkies. Mr. McAllum had the privilege of takin' me and my mammy, or another woman and her two. He took us. So us come to the McAllum plantation to live. It were in Kemper, too, 'bout eight miles from the

Stephensons'. Us come there durin' the war. That were when my mammy marry one of the McAllum niggers. My new pappy went to war with Mr. McAllum and were with him when he were wounded at Mamassas Gab Battle [Manassas]. He brung him home to die—and he done it.

Then the Yankees come through DeKalb, huntin' up cannons and guns and mules. They sho' did eat a heap. Us hid all the best things like silver and drove the stock to the swamp. They didn't burn nothin', but us heard tell of burnin's in Scooba and Meridian. I were a-plowin' a mule, and the Yankees made me take him out. The last I seen of that mule, he were headed for Scooba with three Yankees a-straddle of him.

Times were tight—not a grain of coffee and not much else. When us clothes were plumb wore out, the mist'ess and the nigger womens made us some out of the cotton us had raised. My granny stayed at the loom room all the time. The other womens done the spinnin', and she done the weavin'.

The M&O [Mobile & Ohio Railroad] were a-burnin' wood then. They couldn't get coal. They used tallow pots 'stead of oil. The engineer had to climb out on the engine hisself and 'tend to them tallow pots. They do diff'rent now.

They were such a sca'city of men, they were a-puttin' 'em in the war at sixty-five. But the war end 'fore they call that list.

Mist'ess didn' have nobody to help her durin' the war. She had to do the best she could.

When she heard the niggers talkin' 'bout bein' free, she wore 'em out with a cowhide. She warn't a powerful-built woman, neither. She had to do it herself 'cause warn't nobody to do it for her. They warn't nothin' a nigger could do but stand up and take it.

Some folks treated they slaves mighty bad—put nigger dogs on 'em. All my white folks was good to they slaves, 'cordin' to how good the niggers behaved theyselfs. Course, you couldn't leave no plantation without a pass, or the patteroller'd get you. I ain't countin' that, 'cause that were somethin' ever'body knowed 'forehand.

They were a heap of talk 'bout the Yankees a-givin' every nigger forty acres and a mule. I don't know how us come to hear 'bout it. It just kinda got around. I picked out my mule. All of us did.

Times were mighty tough. Us thought us knowed trouble durin' the war. Us didn't know nothin' 'bout trouble.

They were so many slaves at McAllum's, they had to thin 'em out. Mist'ess put [hired] us out. She sent me to Mr. Scott close to Scooba. I were a most-grown boy by then and could plow pretty good. Come the Surrender, Mr. Scott say, "Sambo, I don't have to pay yo' mist'ess for you no more. I have to pay you if you stay. Niggers is free. You is free." I didn't believe it. I worked that crop out, but I didn't ask for no pay. That didn't seem right. I didn't understand 'bout freedom, so I went home to my old mist'ess. She say, "Sambo, you don' belong to me now."

They bound us young niggers out. They sent me and my brother to a man that were goin' to give us some learnin', 'long with farmin'. His name was Overstreet. Us worked that crop out, but us ain't never seen no speller, nor nothin'. My mammy and me went back to McAllum's and stayed until a man give us a patch in 'turn [return] for us helpin' him on his farm.

I know 'bout the Klu Kluxes. I seen 'em. 'Bout the first time I seen 'em were the last. Ain't nobody know exactly 'bout them Klu Kluxes. Some say it were a spirit that hadn't had no water since the war. Folks that ain't acted right liable to be found most anytime tied up somewheres. The niggers were havin' a party one Sat'day night on Hampton's plantation. Come some men on horses with some kind of scare-face on 'em. They were all wrapped up, disguised. The horses were covered up, too. They call for Miller Hampton. He were one of the Hampton niggers. He been up to somethin'. I don't know what he done, but they say he done somethin' bad. They didn't have no trouble gettin' him, 'cause us were all scared us'd get killed, too. They carried him off with 'em and kilt him that very night.

Us went to DeKalb next day in a drove and ask the white folks to help us. Us buy all the ammunition us could get to take the spirit, 'cause us was a-havin' another party the next week. They didn't come to that party.

I don't know why they don't have no Klu Kluxes now. The spirit still have the same power.

Then I go to work for Mr. Ed McAllum in DeKalb—when I ain't workin' for the Gullys. Mr. Ed were my young marster, you know, and now he were the jailer in DeKalb. I knowed the Chisolms, too. That's how come I seen all I seen and know what ain't never been told. Maybe I's the only one still livin' that were grown and right there and seen it happen.

It started with Mr. John Gully gettin' shot. Now Mr. Gully were a leadin' man 'mongst the white Democratic people in Kemper, but they ain't had much chance for 'bout seven years (I disremember just how long) on 'count of white folks like the Chisolms runnin' ever'thing. Ever'body were sho' it were some of the Chisolm crowd [who shot Gully], but some folks knowed it were that nigger, Walter Riley, that shot Mr. Gully. But ain't nobody ever told the sho' 'nough reason why Walter shot Mr. John Gully.

The Chisolms warn't Yankees, but they warn't white Democratic people. They do say the Chisolms and folks like 'em used to run 'round with the Yankees. Maybe that's how come they was different. Even 'fore the Yankees come, when Mr. Chisolm were on our side, he were loud-mouthed about it.

Mr. John Gully helped Mr. Chisolm get to be judge, but he turned out to be worse than them he had to judge. Mr. Gully and the others made him resign. I reckon maybe that's why he quit bein' a Democratic.

Come the surrender, Mr. Chisolm got to be a big leader on the other side. And he seen to it that a lot of the white Democratic men got kept from votin' and a lot of niggers step up and vote like he told 'em. They was scared not to. So the Chisolms kept gettin' all the big places [elected offices].

Then Mr. Chisolm's brother got hisself 'pointed sheriff and make Mr. Chisolm deputy. That's when he started runnin' things, sho' 'nough. Next thing you know, Mr. Chisolm is sho' 'nough sheriff hisself.

Then he gather all his kinfolk 'round him, and they make out a blacklist. The folks's name that were on it were the ones the Chisolms didn't need. It were talked 'round that the first name on that list were Mr. John Gully's name. A heap o' Klu Kluxes names were on it, too. Mr. Chisolm send the Klu Kluxes' names to the Gov'nor and expect him to do somethin' 'bout runnin' 'em out. Every now and then somebody what's name were on that list would get shot in the back.

'Fore the 'lection come in November—it musta been in '75—the niggers had been a-votin' and doin' ever'thing the Chisolms say. They were still a-harpin' back to that forty acres and a mule they were promised, what they ain't never got. It were turnin' out to be just the same with ever'thing else Mr. Chisolm had been a-promised to give 'em. They ain't never got none of it. The white Democratic folks won that 'lection.

Soon Mr. Chisolm run for somethin' or 'nother and got beat bad. Then he were mad sho' 'nough. He went to Jackson to see the Gov'nor 'bout it. Soon a heap o' white Democratic men in Kemper got arrested for somethin' or 'nother.

Then Mr. John Gully got shot and ever'body were sho' the Chisolms done it. Ever'body were that mad. Chisolm and them had to go to court. But they were slippery as eels, and Walter Riley's name come out. He were a nigger. They give out at the trial that Walter were hired to shoot him [Gully] by the Chisolm folks. That were not the reason, but they was blood 'fore folks' eyes by that time.

It got worse that Sat'day when Mr. Gully were buried. Folks all over Kemper done heard 'bout it by now, and by nine o'clock Sunday mornin', people were a-comin' in over every road that lead to DeKalb. They all had loaded guns. It were on a Sunday when all the killin' happened—I mean, the windin'-up killin'. I were there 'fore a gun were fired. I were there when the first man were wounded.

The colored people had gathered in DeKalb at the Methodist Church. They warn't a gun fired yet. Mr. Henry Gully [John Gully's brother] goes to the colored people's church. He walked in at the front door and took his hat off his head. They were a-packed in the house for preachin'. He walked down the aisle 'til he got in front of the preacher, and he turn sideways and speak: "I want to ask you to dismiss yo' congregation. They is goin' to be some trouble take place right here in DeKalb, and I don't want any colored person to get hurt." The preacher rise to his feet, every nigger in the house were up, and he dismiss 'em.

The town were a-millin' with folks from ever'where. Chisolm and them done got in the jail for safety, and Miss Cornelia Chisolm went backward and forwards to the jail. They thought she were a-carryin' ammunition in her clothes to her father. Mr. McClendon—he were one of 'em [Chisolm's men]—were with her. Some believed he were the one that killed Mr. John Gully.

Well, Mr. McClendon were shot down 'side Miss Cornelia. I seen him when he fell on his face. The man that fired the gun turn him over and say, "Well, us got him." Miss Cornelia run on to the jail, where the bounce [balance] of the family were.

Them outside say, "Boys, it'll never do! They ain't all in there yet. Let's send to Scooba and get Charlie Rosenbaum and John Gilmore to come help they friends. They belongs to that Chisolm crowd, and we want them, too."

So they [Rosenbaum and Gilmore] come [to the jail]. Somebody say, "Let's commence right here." I never seen a battle before, but I sho' seen one then. It were like this: Mr. Cal Hull was the only white Democratic friend Mr. Rosenbaum had. He stood 'twixt his white Democratic friends and Mr. Rosenbaum. He put his arms over Mr. Rosenbaum and say, "Boys, he's a friend of mine. If you kill him, you kill me." Mr. Rosenbaum crawled over to the courthouse wall and squatted down and stayed there. Mr. Hull stood over him, protectin' him. But Mr. John Gilmore make for the jail, and when they open the door for him, the shootin' start. Right then were when Mr. Gilmore got his. Miss Cornelia were struck in the wrist. It mortified [became infected], and after 'while she died from it.

I know I ain't told the sho' 'nough reason Mr. John Gully got killed. Maybe the time done come for the truth to be told. Hope won't nobody think hard of me for tellin'.

Mr. John Gully had a barroom and a clerk—a white man by the name of Bob Dabbs clerked behind that counter. This nigger, Walter Riley, I was a-tellin' you 'bout a while ago, were a-courtin' a yaller [yellow] woman. They warn't so many of 'em in them days. Mr. Dabbs say, "Walter, if I ever catch you walkin' with her [the yellow woman], I'll give you the worst beatin' ever was." Walter were caught with her again. That Friday night he come a-struttin' into the barroom. Mr. Dabbs say, "Come help move these boxes here in the next room." Walter walked in like a nigger will when you ask him to do somethin', and Mr. Dabbs turned the key. "Get 'cross that goods box," he say. "I'll give you what I promised you." Mr. Dabbs got him a piece of plank and burnt Walter up.

All this here were a-goin' on 'bout the time niggers were a-votin' and doin' things 'round white folks. They thought they were pertected by the Chisolm crowd.

The next Friday night, Walter walked right into that barroom again. Mr. Dabbs say, "What you doin' here, nigger?" Walter say, "You 'member what you done to me tonight one week?" And he [Dabbs] say, "Well, what's to it?" Then Walter say, "Well, I come to settle with you." Mr. Dabbs say, "Let me see if I can't hurry you up some," and he reached his hand back to his hip. But 'fore he could draw out [his gun], Walter done run back to the door. They were a chinaberry tree close to the door, and Walter got behind it and fired a pistol. Mr. Dabbs were hit with his arm a-layin' 'cross the counter with his pistol in his hand.

Me and Mr. Ed ('cause he were the jailor), we put him [Dabbs] on a mattress in the room back of the bar, and he died that night. The word just kinda got 'round that some of the Chisolm crowd done killed Mr. Gully's clerk.

Walter run off to Memphis. Mr. Gully were pursuin' after him to ketch him. Walter sho' got tired of him pursuin'. That were the evidence Walter give out 'fore they put the rope on his neck and start him on his way to the gallows, but warn't nobody there to put it down just like it were.

Mr. Sinclair were sheriff by this time, and my young

marster and me went with him to get Walter to take him to the gallows. I can still see Walter now, standin' there with his cap on the back of his head ready to pull down over his eyes after he get there. They were a pow'ful crowd 'round that wagon.

Then come a rider from Scooba, pull a paper from his pocket and hand it to Mr. Sinclair. The Gov'nor had stopped the hangin' 'til the case were investigated. They placed Walter back in jail, and his coffin 'long with him. The lawyers would visit him to get his testimony. They show'd him his coffin all ready and ask him did he do this killin' or not. They want him to say he was hired to do it. They fixed it all up. Warn't nobody to tell just how it were.

I were married by dis time to Laura. She were the nursemaid to Mr. J.H. Currie. She's been dead twenty years now. When the Curries come to Meridian to live, they give me charge of they plantation. I were the leader and stayed and worked the plantation for 'em. They been livin' in Meridian twelve years. I's married now to they cook.

I's got four boys livin'. One son were in the big strike in the automobile plant in Detroit and couldn't come to see me last Christmas. He'll come to see me next year, if I'm still here.

Maybe folks gonna think hard of me for tellin' what ain't never been told before. I been asked to tell what I seen, and I done it.

Editor's note: Mr. McAllum's account of the murder leading up to the violent confrontation outside the DeKalb jail is problematic. Several times he refers to the murder victim as Mr. John Gully. Near the end of the account, he names the murder victim as Bob Dabbs, an employee of John Gully. Regardless of the inconsistency, the account is a gripping example of the violence that plagued the era following the Civil War. A note preceding the narrative in the original transcripts also makes reference to these inconsistencies. It reads: "While this old Negro may be mistaken at some points (the universal failing of witnesses), his impressions are certainly not more involved than the welter of local records. Mrs. Currie [the wife of Mr. McAllum's employer during the latter years of his life] states that if Sam said he saw a thing happen thus, it may be depended upon that he is telling exactly what he really saw."

Lizzie Williams

Age 88

when interviewed in Calhoun City, Mississippi

I's 88 years old the first day of this past June. I's born in Grenada County, five miles this side of Graysport.

My mammy was Mary Williams, and I had fourteen brothers and sisters, but theys all dead now 'cept me.

My marsa was Captain Jack Williams, and Captain Jack's mammy, Miss Lorena Williams, was my missus. Captain Jack never did marry. He owned 'bout 1,400 acres land, ten or fifteen grown nigger men what was called the plow hands, and lots of fifteen- and sixteen-year-old boys 'sides the women and chillun.

Back in them days, we lived in little log house daubed with mud and had dirt floors. They was covered with boards and weighted down with plank to keep 'em from blowin' off. We slept on a quilt spread on the ground for our bed.

My job back in them days was to weave, spin thread, run the loom. Durin' crop time, I plowed and hoed in the field. My mammy was a regular field hand.

Marsa was good to us niggers. He never would whip us. The overseers was a Mr. Gentry, Mr. Vanvoosa, and Mr. Hamilton, and they would sho' get 'hold of us if we didn't work to suit 'em.

They didn't give us nothing much to eat. They was a trough out in the yard what they poured the mush and milk in, and us chillun and the dogs would all crowd 'round it and eat together. Us chillun had homemade wooden paddles to eat with, and we sho' had to be in a hurry 'bout it 'cause the dogs would get it all if we didn't. Heap of times we'd eat coffee grounds for bread. Sometimes we'd have biscuits made out of what was called the seconds. The white folks always got the firsts. The slaves didn't have no gardens, but old missus give us onion tops out of her garden.

We sho' didn't have 'nuff clothes to wear back in slavery days neither. The old shoemaker on the place made every nigger one pair a shoes a year, and if he wore 'em out he didn't get no more. I's been to the field many a frosty mornin' with rags tied 'round my feet.

The overseer sent us to the field every mornin' by

four o'clock, and we stayed 'til after dark. By the time cotton was weighted up and supper cooked and ate, it was midnight when we'd get to bed a heap of times. These overseers saw that every nigger got his 'mount of cotton. The grown ones had to pick six hundred, seven hundred, and eight hundred pounds a day, and the fourteen- and fifteen-year-old ones had to pick four hundred and five hundred pounds.

Warn't much sickness back in slavery days 'cept when the women was confined, and ole Missus and a nigger woman on the place tended to such cases. I 'member once my mamma had to wash standin' in sleet and snow knee-deep when her baby was just three days old. It made her so sick she almost died. Ole Missus generally got Jerusalem weed out of the woods and made syrup out of it to get rid of the worms in the chillun. She'd give calomel [chamomile] in 'lasses when we needed cleanin' out.

I's seen heap of niggers sold. The white folks would put pieces of quilts in the men's britches to make 'em look like big fine niggers and bring lots of money.

I seed one woman named Nancy durin' the war what could read and write. When her master, Oliver Perry, found this out he made her pull off naked, whipped her, and then slapped hot irons all over her. Believe me, that nigger didn't want to read and write no more.

I's seen nigger women that was fixin' to be confined [give birth] do somethin' the white folks didn't like. They would dig a hole in the ground just big 'nough for her stomach, make her lie face down, and whip her on the back to keep from hurtin' the child. Lots of times the women in that condition would be plowin' and hit a stump. The plow jump and hurt the child to where they would lose it. Law me, such a whippin' as they would get!

We went to preachin' at the white folks' church. The preacher would preach to the white folks first, then he'd call the niggers in and preach to us. He wouldn't read the Bible. He'd say, "Obey yo' missus and yo' marsa." One old nigger didn't have no better sense than to shout on it once.

When niggers died you could hear someone goin' on the road singin': "Hark, from the Tomb the Mournful Sound."

I's seen the patterollers whip niggers. They would always put his head under the rail fence and whip him from the back. We used to sing a song like this: "Run, nigger, run. The patterollers will catch you 'tis almost day."

When the war was over, Marsa come told us niggers we was free but said if we'd stay on with him, the cotton money would be divided out between us niggers. Sho' 'nough, Marsa sold that cotton and 'fore he could divide it out, his sister, Miss Bitha, stole it. Finally he got a little of it and give it to the niggers. Some of 'em took it and ain't been back since. We stayed on there three years. Finally Captain Jack give his niggers land, and they just stayed on with him.

My first husband was Bob Pittman, and our only child died. My next one was George Jean, and our only child died. Then I married Hilliard Williams, and we had fourteen chillun and raised 'em on Captain Jack's place. Only four livin' now. They is day laborers, a preacher, and a farmer. Me and my ole man lived together fifty years. He died in 1927. We was the founders of the colored Methodist church at Big Creek.

Henri Necaise

Age 105 when interviewed
at his home near Nicholson, Mississippi

I was born in Harrison County, nineteen miles from Pass Christian, 'long the ridge road from the swamp to Wolf River. My marster was Ursan Ladnier. The mist'ess's name was Popone. Us was all French. My father was a white man, Anatole Necaise. I knowed he was my father, 'cause he used to call me to him and tell me I was his oldest son.

I never knowed my mother. I was a slave, and my mother was sold from me and her other chilluns. They told me when they sold her, my sister was a-holdin' me in her arms. She was standin' behind the big house peekin' 'round the corner and seen the last of her mother. I seen her go, too. They tell me I used to go to the gate a-huntin' for my mammy. I used to sleep with my sister after that.

Just lemme study a little, and I'll tell you 'bout the big house. It was 'bout sixty feet long, built of hewed logs, in two parts. The floors was made of clay—they didn't have lumber for floors then. Us lived right close to the big house, in a cabin. To tell the truth, the fact of the business is, my marster took care of me better'n I can take care of myself now.

When us was slaves, Marster tell us what to do. He say, "Henri, do this. Do that." And us done it. Then us didn't have to think where the next meal comin' from, or the next pair of shoes or pants. The grub and clothes give to us was better'n I ever gets now.

Lemme think and count. My marster didn't have a lot of slaves. There was one, two, three, four of us slaves. I was the stockholder. I tended the sheep and cows and such like. My marster didn't raise no big crops—just corn and garden stuff. He had a heap of cattle. They could run out in the big woods then, and so could the sheeps. He sold cattle to New Orleans and Mobile, where he could get the best price. That's the way folks does now, ain't it? They sells wherever they can get the most money.

They didn't give me money, but, you see, I was a slave. They sho' give me ever'thing else I need—clothes and shoes. I always had a-plenty to eat; better'n I can get now.

My marster was a Catholic. One thing I can thank them godly white folks for, they raise me right. They taught me out of God's word, "Our Father, which art in heaven." Ever'body oughta know that prayer.

My mist'ess knowed how to read and write. I don't know 'bout the marster. He could keep store anyway. Us all spoke French in them days. I near 'bout forget all the songs us used to sing. They was all in French anyway, and when you don't speak no French for 'bout 60 years, you just forget it.

I's knowed slaves to run away, and I's seen 'em whipped. I seen good marsters and mean ones. They was good slaves and mean ones. But to tell the truth, if they told a slave to do anything, then he just better do it.

I was big 'nough in the Civil War to drive five yoke of steers to Mobile and get grub to feed the women and chillun. Some of the mens was a-fightin' and some was a-runnin' and hidin'. I was a slave, and I had to do what they told me. I carried grub into the swamp to men, but I never knowed what they was a-hidin' from.

My old marster had four sons, and the youngest one went to the war and was killed.

The Yankees come to Pass Christian. I was there and seen 'em. They come up the river and tore up things as they went along.

I was 31 years old when I was set free. My marster didn't tell us 'bout bein' free. The way I found it out, he started to whip me once, and the young marster up and says, "You ain't got no right to whip him now, he's free." Then Marster turned me loose.

It was them carpetbaggers that 'stroyed the country. They went and turned us loose, just like a passel of cattle, and didn't show us nothin' or give us nothin'. They was acres and acres of land not in use, and lots of timber in this country. They shoulda give each one of us a little farm and let us get out timber and build houses. They oughta put a white marster over us to show us and make us work, only let us be free 'stead of slaves. I think that woulda been better than turnin' us loose like they done.

I left my marster and went over to the Jordan River, and there I stayed and worked. I saved my money and that give me a start. I never touched it 'til the year was winded up. To tell the truth, the facts of the matter is, it was my marster's kinfolk I was workin' for.

I bought a schooner with that money and carried charcoal to New Orleans. I done this for 'bout two years, and then I lost my schooner in a storm off of Bay St. Louis.

After I lost my schooner, I come here and got married. This was in 1875, and I was 43 years old. That was my first time to marry. I's got that same wife today. She was born a slave, too. I didn' have no chillun, but my wife did. She had one gal. She lives in Westonia and is the mammy of ten chillun. I's got a lot of grandchillun.

I never did believe in no ghost and hoodoos and charms.

I never did look for to get nothin' after I was free. I had in my head to get me eighty acres of land and homestead it. As for the gov'ment making me a present of anything, I never thought 'bout it. But just now I needs it.

I did get me this little farm, forty acres, but I bought it and paid for it myself. I got the money by workin' for it. When I come to this country, I dug wells and built chimneys and houses. Once I dug a well 27 feet and come to a coal bed. I went through the coal and found water. That was on the Jordan River. That clay and chimney and this here house has been built for 52 years. I's still livin' in 'em. They's mine. One acre, I give to the Lord for a graveyard and a church house. I wants to be buried there.

I raises a garden and gets the old-age 'sistance [assistance]. It ain't 'nough to buy grub and clothes for me and the old woman and pay taxes, so us just has to get 'long the best us can with the white folks' help.

It ain't none of my business 'bout whether the niggers is better off free than slaves. I don't know 'cept 'bout me. I was better off then. I did earn money after I was free, but after all, you know money is the root of all evil. That is what the Good Book say.

I's gettin' mighty old now, but I used to be pretty spry. I used to go 60 miles out on the Gulf of Mexico, as a 'terpreter [interpreter] on them big ships that come from France. That was 'fore I done forgot my French talk what I was raised to speak.

Editor's Note: The Wolf River territory in Harrison County where Henri Necaise lived as a slave was the scene of early Catholic missions and settled primarily by French Catholics. This may explain his account of carrying food to men hiding in the swamp—many of the area's French Catholics refused to support either side during the Civil War.

Clara C. Young

Age unknown when interviewed
at her home in Monroe County, Mississippi

I don't know when I was born, but I do know that I's seventeen years old when I was first sold. They put me and my brother up on the auction block at the same time. He brung $1400.00, but I disremembers exactly what they paid for me. Warn't that much, for big strong men brung more than women and gals.

I was born in Huntsville, Alabama, and my mammy and pappy was name Silby and Sharper Conley. They took the last name from the old marster, who owned 'em. I lived there with 'em 'til the chillun drew their parts [took their inheritance] and us was 'vided [divided] out. While I was with old Marster, he let Miss Rachel— that was his wife—have me for the house. She learned me how to cook and wait on the table. I declare, she call me her very smartest gal! Sometimes, though, I wouldn't come right quick-like when she ring the bell for me, and she'd start ringin' it harder and harder. I knowed then she was mad. When I'd get there, she'd fuss at me and turn my dress up and whup me—not hard, 'cause she warn't so strong—but I'd holler some.

They had a nigger woman to teach all the house darkies how to read and write. I learned how to sign my name and got as far as b-a-k-e-r in the Blue Back Speller.

Marse Conley and Miss Rachel had four chillun: Miss Mary, Miss Alice, Miss Willie, and Marse Andrew. When the time come, they give me to Marse Andrew. He carried me and the rest out to Texas, where he thought he'd go and get rich. We never stayed long, though, for lots of the niggers runned 'way to the Free State [non-slaveholding states]. Marse Andrew didn't like that.

It was when he brought us back to Huntsville that I was sold. All the white folks was gettin' scared they was going to lose they slaves, and there was a powerful lot of nigger sellin' goin' on then. Marse Ewing bought me from him [Andrew Conley] and carried me to his plantation near Aberdeen, Mississippi. Then I started to work in the field with the rest of the hands. The overseer we had was right mean to us when we didn't work our rows as fast as the others. Sometimes he whup us, women and all. When he did that some of us 'most nigh always tell the marster and he'd jump on the overseer and tell him to lay off the women and the chillun. They was always sorta thoughtful of us, and we loved ole Marster.

I heard tell one time, though, of the headman (he was a nigger) and the overseer whuppin' one of my cousins 'til she bled. She was just seventeen years old and was in the family way for the first time and couldn't work as hard as the rest. Next mornin' after that, she died. The headman told the rest if they said anything 'bout it to the marster he'd beat 'em to death, too. Ever'body kept quiet, and the marster never knowed.

We worked hard in the field all day, but when dark come we'd all go to the quarters. After supper we'd set 'round and sing and talk. We had good food to eat 'cause most of us had our gardens, and the quarter's cook would cook what we wanted if we brung it to her. Durin' the last years 'fore the Surrender, we didn't have much to eat though, and made out best we could.

The most fun we had was at our meetin's. We had them most every Sunday, and they lasted way into the night. The preacher I liked best was named Matthew Ewing. He was a comely nigger, black as night, and he sho' could read outen his hand. He never learned no real readin' and writin', but he sho' knowed his Bible. He would hold his hand out and make like he was readin' and preach the purtiest preachin' you ever heard. The meetin's last from early in the mornin' 'til late at night.

When dark come, the menfolks would hang up a wash pot, bottom upwards, in the little brush church house us had so's it'd catch the noise and the overseer wouldn't hear us singin' and shoutin'. They didn't mind us meetin' in the daytime, but they thought if we stayed up half the night we wouldn't work so hard the next day, and that was the truth.

You shoulda seen some of the niggers get religion. The best way was to carry them to a cemetery and let them stand over a grave. They would start singin' and shoutin' 'bout seein' fire and brimstone. Then they would sing some mo' and look plum sanctified.

When us had our big meetin', there'd always be some darkies from the plantations come 'round. They would have to slip off 'cause they marsters was afraid they would get hitched up with some other black boy or gal on the other plantation. Then they would have to buy or sell a nigger 'fore you could get any work outen 'em.

We never knowed much 'bout the war, 'cept that we didn't have as much to eat or wear, and the white menfolks was all gone. Then, too, old Miss cried a lot of the time.

The Yankees came 'round after the war and told us we's free. We shouted and sang and held a big celebration for a few days. Then we got to wonderin' 'bout what good it did us. It didn't feel no diff'ent. We all loved our marster and missus and stayed on with them just like nothin' had happened. The Yankees tried to get some of the men to vote, too, but not many did 'cause they was scared of the Ku Kluxers. They would come at night all dressed up like ghosts and scare us all. We didn't like the Yankees anyway. They warn't good to us. When they left us, we would always sing that little song what go like this:

> Old mister Yankee, think he is so gran'
> With his blue coattail a-draggin' on the groun'!

I stayed on with old Marster after the Surrender with the rest, 'til I met Joshua. Joshua Young was his name, and he belonged to the Youngs what lived out at Waverly. I moved out there with him after we married. We didn't have no big weddin' 'cause there warn't much money then. We had a preacher, though, and then went 'long just like we'd always been married.

Josh, he's been dead for a long time now, but we had a good life out at Waverly. Many a night, we stood outside the parlor door and watch the white folks at their big dances and parties. The folks was powerful nice to us, and we raised a passel of chillun out there. All of them 'cept three be dead now. Of those left, George is the oldest. He's a bricklayer, carpenter, preacher, and 'most anything else he decides to call hisself. He's got 19 or 20 chillun. Edith ain't got so many. She lives up North. I lives with my other daughter and her girl. I named her after my sisters. Her name is Anna Luvenia Hulda Larissa Jane Bell Young McMillan. That last name is her married name. Janie Mae Prince, that's my granddaughter that takes care of me and her mammy, counted up my livin' chillun and grandchillun. She says there is 54 of them in all. There may be more than that now, but anyways there is five generations livin'.

Isaac Potter

Age unknown when interviewed
in his home near D'Lo, Mississippi

My first master was Jim Crowder, who bought my father and mother from Yankee slave traders, who had captured 'em and brung 'em over here from Africa and sold 'em to the Southern farmers. The Crowder plantation was big. I don't know how many acres, but there was 'round seventy or seventy-five slaves. This was in Rankin County, near Pelahatchee. His home was one of them big two-story antebellum homes, with a big kitchen and dinin' room built of logs in long rows back 'way from the main part where they kept cooks busy a-feedin' and cookin' for the slaves. The slaves' cottages was built of logs in long rows back of Marse's house. Us lived in them but ate in the big kitchen. The slave workers was fed first. Later the chillun was called in and fed.

Our mothers would all be out workin' and sometimes us chillun would get into mischief. As for myself, I always did crave a little fun and mix play along with my work. Sometimes I would catch it. One of my first duties was to feed the chickens, which was raised by the hundreds. They would send me with big buckets of feed to the chicken's yard. I did enjoy taking long sticks or big rocks and killin' 'em. This was real fun to me. At first I was afraid to kill many of 'em, then I got braver and braver and killed more and more. I was the big giant, and they was little men. I'd feed 'em and kill one man. Then I feel big and kill another, and so on like that. I forgot ever'thing 'til I hear Marse's gal, Miss Mary Ann's, voice behind me say, "Now I's caught you." My hair stood straight up. I looked at my kill. It looked like a thousand. I didn't know there could be that many dead chickens in the world. She count 'em. I had killed twenty-five.

She whipped me. I warn't used to bein' whipped much, and I slipped off in the woods 'fraid old Missus would whip me, too. They hunted through the woods all night for me with big torches. Some of the slaves found me and told me Missus said she warn't going to whip me. I went home 'bout the crack of day.

My master died and 'bout a year later, Missus married Master Gilbert. Us like Marse Gilbert 'cause he was good to us. He didn't live long 'fore he died, too. Missus married again. This man was named Potter. This put me serving under three masters.

I always did like to do what I seed other folks do. From a small chile I had enjoyed acting out things. I wish I had been one of them actor niggers. One day when I was 'bout eight years old, me and my brother had run out of nothin' to amuse us. It was a long, cold, winter day. Us was setting 'round a big fire in the cabin. The fire burned low to a deep-red bed of coals. This gave me an idea. I told my brother for us to play like us was Milly, the cook, with the big apron and cap and ever'thing. Us stirred the coals and was ready, all but the big aprons. Us didn't know what to do 'bout that, when us thought of two gunny sacks out in the wood-shed. Us got 'em and tied 'em 'round us necks 'til they reached our toes—the very thing us needed. I had more than my brother, for I tied his in a bow, while he tied mine in a hard knot.

Us went to work, just like Aunt Milly. We put bread in a skillet on the coals and covered sweet potatoes in the hot ashes. Then we raked up some coals and fried us some ham. When the meal was finished, us was going to take the aprons off. Brother, he reached up and give his a pull, and the bow come untied, but mine was tied so it just wouldn't come loose. Us tried 'til we saw us couldn't make it. Us decided to stick fire to it and burn it off. Brother set fire to it at my feet, and the fire blazed all over that fuzzy sack like lightnin'. I run and screamed to ole Missus. That is why my face, hands, and body is all scarred up today.

In slave days, if us wanted to go somewhere off the plantation, us had to get a pass from our master, then us had to get in by a certain time. If us failed to be back the patterollers would find it out and bring us in. Sometimes us would visit each other and set 'round a while and talk or go huntin'. That is what I want to do most of all. In them days there was lots of game in the swamps.

Us had dances, too. That's when us had a grand time, with the fiddles and guitars a-playin'. At times the niggers would tie up and fight. If they hurt a slave, he was scared to go home, for the owner would get riled up if one of his slaves got hurt or crippled up. At these frolics we would be havin' such a merry time us would forget when to go home. They always had a big fire burnin' to see by. When the patrol rode up to take us in, we would fight 'em off with hot coals. Dozens of niggers would be slingin' fire as hard and fast as they could throw it. The patrol riders would just naturally have to run.

When I was a slave, and for years afterwards, I had the superstition of my race, but I's done learned better than to believe a heap of that stuff. But just before the war to free us, we had the coldest winter that I believe has ever been on the face of the earth. The deepest snows would come, wrappin' up ever'thing, and stay on the ground for days. The ponds and lakes would freeze over with thick coats of ice. It got so cold 'til the pigeons begin to fly north in such big droves that they looked like big clouds. One day us slaves saw a cloud of 'em flyin' over us. We took long flint guns and begin to shoot 'em. I helped pick up a cotton basketful. When the war come on, us believed all that to be a warnin'.

'Fore I learned better, I saw more ghosts than any nigger alive. I's run many a mile from haints. When I had to pass a graveyard at night, I'd pull my hat over my face and hold it as tight as I could and run 'til I'd be plumb out of breath. One night I saw a sure-enough ghost. It was a headless woman dressed in black, a-walkin' 'round. I like to run plumb out of the country. Another haint kept me in a old field all night one time. I had been to see my gal and was going to cut through a old field [on the way] home. The moon was a-shinin' bright. I looked up and saw a tall, white ghost ahead of me. My hair stood straight out and sizzled. I was scared to move, then I bowed over and that ghost bowed, too. Each time I moved, it did, too. I just lay down and be right still so that ghost would be still. I stayed there for hours, for everytime I would stir, that ghost stir, too. I decided I would talk to it. I say, "Now if you will let me alone, I will let you alone." I stood trembling and told that ghost ever'thing I could think of, when I happened to notice that all the time it was my shadder [shadow] against a tall stump. I ain't believed in no ghost since.

When the war come on, I reckon I'd join it. I worked in the camp for a long time. I was already trained to look after horses and be handy at ever'thing in general. I enjoyed watchin' the soldiers drill and the sham battles. I was a-takin' it all in. Soon I knowed how to march and draw the gun. I never could understand why the soldiers could be so cheerful knowing they might get killed any time. They would sing and dance and joke all the time, right up to the time they was called to battle. I've saw 'em come in after a hard battle, when the Northern soldiers would be campin' near, they would go to each other's camps and swap coffee and tobacco. They would laugh and wrestle and have the biggest time. When they would part for the night, they would say to each other, "We'll give you hell tomorrow."

'Long toward the end of the war, the Southern soldiers got so hungry. The [northern] cavalrymen had come through and destroyed ever'thing to eat. I have seen big army wagons with them big wheels run over big frogs, mashing them flat as a rag. The soldiers come 'long and shake the dust off and eat 'em. They would eat horseflesh. I have eaten it a number of times and liked it.

After the war ended and us was freed, us had a hard time. After a few years of hirin' out, I settled on a small farm and got married. I am now livin' with my second wife. My first wife and all my chillun, but one, is dead. I's old and nearly blind. The government is takin' care of me, and I wants to stay here as long as I can.

George Washington Miller

Age approximately 81 when interviewed
at his home in Clay County, Mississippi

I was born in Spartanburg, South Carolina, on March 15, 1856.

My ma's name was Emaline Hobby of Spartanburg, South Carolina, and my pa's name was Washington Young of the same place. I had one brother, Walter Silas Miller, and two sisters, Calline and Florence Miller, all of Spartanburg.

My ma was sold to the Youngs by the Hobbys, and a daughter married Marster Pickney Wyatt Miller, a doctor. One peculiar thing about the family was that all the Miller men had a "W" in their name, each adopting the name Wyatt. W.J. Miller, the ex-state treasurer of Mississippi, is a son of Mars Pickney Wyatt Miller, my old marster.

All I know about our life happened after the Millers moved and brought us to Batesville, Panola County, Mississippi, before the war. My ma didn't come, because she never could get along with Marse Miller. He had her sold to a man named Ducket in Laurens County. How she ever got to Mississippi, I just don't know. But she got to Batesville the first year after the war and found my pa and married again.

When the Northern army got as near as Memphis, Dr. P.W. Miller got so uneasy about the Yankees that he sent us children, the Millers and Youngs, back to South Carolina in wagons, trying to keep the Yankees from stealing us. There were no railroads, as all were torn up. The doctor took us to his mother's plantation, where we had kin. I was just old enough to help do little jobs such as drive the sheep and cows. "Miss Sally" [P.W. Miller's mother] was good to me and cared for us well. Not many slaves there in South Carolina knew there was a war going on, and we could tell them about the raids on plantations back in Mississippi. To see great armies of men in uniforms was fun for us children. We craved to see it. I was always loyal to the Millers because I loved 'em. I didn't want to leave, even when my ma came for me.

The doctor's brother came to South Carolina for his own white children after the war. He had a wagon and three mules that he had carried back to save. One of us had died, but three of us was brought back to Panola in this wagon, along with the white folks. Among the white folks was a lawyer named Mason Anderson of Spartanburg, the first lawyer I ever knew about. I understand his family is prominent in the state of Mississippi.

We wore good clothes, which were spun and woven on the plantation. Our shoes was made by plantation shoemakers. I always attributed my rheumatism to the fact that one winter I couldn't get shoes until very late. I never did wear any short pants. Ours were long, like the men. I must of had good pockets, because when I started back to Mississippi, T.W. Miller gave me a five-dollar bill, which I still had when we got to Panola. We were on the road about six weeks. Some places we traveled was so strong with stink from battles fought and dead bodies left, we had to hold our noses.

We came right through Warm Springs, Georgia. I paid some attention to the different kinds of folks, because I like to be informed. A Mr. Bill Stone, who lived on Talahatchie River at Batesville, made a practice of having "nigger hounds" to catch runaway niggers.

The Miller plantation in Mississippi was a half section. He only had three grown negro men and three or four women, but the Youngs, who was the father-in-law and lived right in Panola, or what's present Batesville, owned 80 slaves.

A plantation bell called everybody to daylight. The field hands were at work from "sun to sun." I never saw a slave whipped, but I've heard that 500 lashes were given for stealing or being lazy. In South Carolina I've heard of Negroes who wanted money so bad they would even shear the sheep in the winter and sell the wool. They would be whipped most of the time by the justice of the peace. When a Negro was sold, he was put on a block. The children in South Carolina were scared when a stranger came around, for they thought they were "speculators" and wanted to buy them. They would scatter and hide like young partridges. I saw one slave chained, after I was brought back to Mississippi, because he was a runaway. He just wouldn't be whipped, and he wouldn't work. His old master "belled" him. The blacksmith so made the bells and attachment that it couldn't be taken off. As he walked or rode, the bells would ring.

My white folks had a "refugee," who came out of Memphis to teach any of us who wanted to learn. I just got sick when she left us, because I did want to learn.

I saw baptizing after we came back to Mississippi at Panola, at "Sinners Campground." The Negroes and whites all went to the same church, and white preachers did the baptizing. His name was Middleton, a big slave owner. I remember seeing him baptize several white and black, and my father was one of the Negroes. Most of the churches, being white, the spirituals were not sung. My favorites are common hymns, short and long meter.

I've known of Negroes who ran away to get to Ohio,

where they would be free. Our group always hoped and talked of being freed. I always listened, because I wanted to learn. They would tell stories almost in a whisper about being "free."

I was in the Carolinas when news of freedom came at the death of Lincoln. We was looking for it, because the Confederates had so many backsats [setbacks]. I remembers about Sherman's march through Georgia. When we come back to Mississippi, we saw garrisons of soldiers on the way. Nobody knew their status. Everything was unsettled. A Yankee advisor told our group of grown Negroes to go back to the marsters, and they would give them employment.

I came to West Point with my mother, Emaline, the first year after the war and worked about home in her patches and helped keep her boardinghouse. Sometimes she hired us out to chop cotton. I started at once to school in West Point in a schoolroom on the Cochran plantation, four miles from town. The teacher was named John Williams.

There was a white man from Indiana, Glen Valley, twelve miles from Indianapolis, boarding with my mother and teaching the Negroes. There was a notice put on my mother's gate. On the notice was a red heart with a sword through it, showing that he must quit teaching or his life was in danger. He left and went back to Indiana.

One night the Ku Klux raided the town in all their

regalia. We colored folks were at the church near the cemetery on a Saturday night. We boys ran out and followed them laughing. They come by the church. Captain Shattuck, a good Yankee, advised the Negroes to behave and settle down, and believe in their own white folks.

I married Ellen Baptist, a house girl of Mrs. Baptist of West Point. We married in the home of Mrs. Tittle, a sister of Mr. Jack Baptist, where my wife was serving. Isaac Mosely, a colored preacher, married us right in the Tittles' parlor. Only four colored people were there. We two [he and his wife] are the only ones now living who were present, white or black. We have had five children, three girls and two boys. Only one is dead. Two of the girls is teachers. One son, William Tell, is dead, leaving no family. Carris, who's married and lives in St. Louis, was a trained nurse. George M. Jr. is a world war veteran and lives in Toledo, Ohio.

Emily Dixon

Age approximately 108 when intervewed
in her home near D'Lo, Mississippi

If you wants my story, I's going to tell it just like it
is. No use tellin' no lies, or polishin' up nothin'. My
mother was raised by her mistress and nursed by one of
the slave women. Her mother was sold away from her
when she was a little baby. My mother loved our mistress. When she died, I can recollect yet how ma
whooped and hollered. Ole Missus was kinder to me
than Ma was. She used to make her quit whipping me,
for Ma beat me too hard. The only time Missus ever
whipped me was with a straw.

We lived in a small cottage in Marster's yard. He
was some kind of officer, I guess, as he kept the jail and
fed the prisoners. That was one of my first duties, was

takin' food to them. The jailhouse won't good like they is now. Somebody was always breakin' out. That stirred up a heap of excitement. The men would get out the horses and run 'em, hunt 'em, and shoot 'em all over the woods.

My first play that I can recollect was 'round the old hickory-nut trees. They gives a child a heap of pleasure. Did you ever take time to think just what a hickory-nut tree is to chillun? There's the shade to play under, the tree to climb, the big limbs to hang swings from, the leaves to pin together with pine straw to make dresses and hats, the nuts to eat and throw at each other. If you all wants to fight, I's hit many a little nigger on the head with 'em. Then you can hide 'hind the trunks in playin' hide-and-seek, or have it for the base. I have had my fun under the ole hickory-nut tree.

Marster had a heap of horses and mules that made up my next work as a slave gal. When I growed up a bit, me and my brother had to drive the mules to water and to and from the pastures. We crossed the stream wherever the mules did. If there warn't no foot log, we waded. If it was too deep, us would swim. On one of these trips, I was just a strip of a gal. Me and my brother and the mules was going through a dark swamp 'bout dusk. The clouds was a-hangin' low and heavy. There didn't seem to be no air. Us could hear the rollin' thunder comin' nearer, the lightnin' was a-flashin' fast, lightin' up the woods, then leavin' 'em darker and darker. Us was a-getting scared. The mules had sensed a comin' storm and had trotted on and left us. Me and brother got to lookin' back and wonderin' what was ever'where. A owl hooted. A big, black bird flew low over our heads (which was a bad sign). The bird flew shriekin' on deeper in the woods. Then it thundered loud and rumbly. A drop or two of rain fell on us. Right then and there, us heard a ghost. Yes, us did hear it. I knowed us did. It was a-walkin' quick and loud. Us looked back and us hastened up, but never could see it. But the first thing us knowed, it seemed to be a-walkin' all 'round us. Us sho' did run so fast no ghost could catch us. Us run a mile 'fore us dared to stop. Now then, that's the only ghost I ever did see, and I just heard it.

I was a spirited chap. Me and my brother would fight when the other chillun meddled with us. One thing I was a bit curious 'bout was my clothes. I never did want any of the rest to wear my dresses, or wanted 'em to make me wear anybody else's dress. If any of the chillun wore my dress, I catch 'em off and me and brother would fight 'em. If they tole on us, us fight 'em again.

During the slave time, us had to work long hard hours in the cotton and corn fields. When the war come on, us had to walk miles to spin and knit. On Sundays us would get together in the woods and have worship. Us could go to the white folks' church but us wanted to go where we could sing all the way through and hum 'long and shout. You all know, just turn loose like.

When I growed up to be a young slave gal, I worked hard but I had a good time going with the boys. I walked 'bout with 'em, went to dances and danced with 'em. I thought a heap of times I was in love but was 'fraid to get married 'cause I feared one or the other of us might be sold. Then I never wanted no man a-beatin' me up, so I raised my six chillun without the fears and worries of bein' married. I'd seen heartbroken wives stand by with babies in their arms while their husbands was led up to the crossroads with others, where hundreds of speculators would be a-waitin' to buy 'em. Long lines of men, women, boys, and gals would be drove up and sold.

My marster raised sheep. When the dogs killed one, us had to pull the wool off the dead sheep. Sometimes they had been dead for days and would be so sickenin' 'til I went to smokin' a pipe. The smoke kept us from gettin' so sick. I has been using tobacco and snuff since long before the war. I gets a heap of pleasure and company from usin' 'em. I likes my pipe best.

After the war was over and us was freed, I homestead that place here near D'Lo. I's been farmin' ever since and workin' among the white folks. My chillun is all married and away, what's not dead. I lives here by myself.

Ebenezer Brown

Age 85 when interviewed
at his home in Amite County, Mississippi

I is now eighty-five years old. I was born 'bout twelve miles south of Liberty, on the road that goes from Liberty to Jackson, Louisiana, on Mr. Bill McDowell's place. That was a big farm. Marse Bill was mighty tough on his slaves. I was just a boy, but I will never forget how he whupped his slaves. I can name every one of his slaves. There was Viney—she done the cookin'. Zias was a field hand, and he drive the carriage. My uncle, Irwin, he fed the hosses. He was a bad nigger and got whupped for stealin' all the time. Jim was the rice beater, and he beat the rice every Friday. Sara was a field hand. Relia work in the field and milked and had to go to the cowpen barefooted. Her feet got frostbit and that made her cripple. Hager was a field hand, and Peggy was a field hand. After Relia got crippled, Peggy helped milk. Monday was a field hand, but he was bad 'bout runnin' 'way from home, and the patteroller would get him. Patience, that was my mammy, she milked and worked in the field. Then there was some big chilluns that helped in the field, and we all had to work 'round the house. There was Tom, a nigger boy 'bout my age. We played together and done work together.

Marse Bill had a big, fine two-story house. It was white, and the front of it was to the west. On the north side of the house was a dug well, sixty-five-feet deep. It had a pulley over it and two buckets. When one bucket would come up, the other would go down. My, that was cold water, but the buckets was heavy. The garden was on the south side of the house, and the pigeon house was on the northwest side of the big house, just over the carriage house.

Marse Bill's wife was named Miss Hester, and their chilluns was named young Marse Russ. He was grown and toted a big whip all the time. He helped Marse Bill look after the darkies in the field. And then there was young Marse Tom, and Miss Lizzie, and Miss Mary, and Miss Ella, and Miss Ethel, and Miss Dulcie, and that was all.

Marse Bill had two brothers. One was named Tom, and one was named John. Mr. Tom was a mighty rich man. He used to loan money. One time Marse Bill put me on his big, fine black pony named "Snap" and give me a note and sent me to Mr. Tom's. When I got there, Mr. Tom said, "What's the matter with Bill now?" Then I give him the note. He said, "Lord, Jesus Christ, peas and rice. That is what Bill is always wantin'—money! money! money!" He give me the money and put me back on the black hoss and sent me home.

As a child, I played in the yard with another black boy named Tom Hardin, but they didn't 'low [allow] for us to play much. We shot chinaberries from a popgun, and we made the shots hit the other chaps and would get whupped for it. We done that all the time. We toted in wood for Viney, so she could cook. She cooked in a big fireplace with racks in the chimbly. Then we had to pick up the eggs every day. We had to pick up the plums from under the trees and tote 'em in baskets to the hogs. Then we picked up the peaches and apples that fell off the trees and toted them to the hogs. That made the hogs fat. Then Marse Bill made cider out of the apples, and that was good. Then I had to churn every other day. That churn was 'bout three feet high, and it had a long handle dasher. I had to stand there and work that handle up and down 'til the butter would come. When I seed the little lumps of butter stickin' on the handle, I would take my finger and wipe it off and then suck my finger. But I darsn't let old Mist'ess see me do that. If she caught me doin' it, I would get a whuppin'.

Tom and me had to sweep the yard. Every Sat'day we had what you call "brush-brooms," and we brushed them leaves up in a pile and put them in a basket and toted 'em to a pen behin' the barn and there let 'em rot.

I's going to tell you 'bout my grandmammy. Her name was Dorcas, and she was born in Virginia. A slave trader brung her to Liberty, and Marse Bill seed her and said she was a husky gal. He bought her 'fore they had time to put her on the block. She took up with a slave, that 'longed [belonged] to Mr. Landon Lea, named Jare Avenger. They was my grandmammy and grandpappy. She was old and lived in a log house down the hillside. All she could do was to wash and iron and mind the clothes. Sometimes she work in the loom room. Grandpap stayed over to Mr. Lea's, but after they was set free he come to live at Marse Bill's with grandmammy. My mammy was their chile. Her name was Patience.

My pappy was named Dan. He was born in South Carolina and brung to Liberty and put on the block. Two people wanted him, but Marse Bill said he would give more than they. The bossman said Marse Bill could have him. He brung him home and said, "Patience, I brung you a husband. Go live with him." That was the way they got married. There was no preacher them days to marry you.

My pappy was a carpenter and work in the field and

done the buildin' that was done on the place. He drive the ox team to Osyka to get sugar and flour, and he always had to grease the wagon with tar. That would make it run easy.

Marse Bill had no overseer that I remember. He and young Marse Russ toted the whip and would ride over the field and make the slaves work. They would sure whup if that work wasn't done. Then Marse Bill had a old poll parrot that he put on a limb in the field sometimes, and that parrot would tell who it was that didn't work. Marse Bill would tie them slaves and whup hard, and all the slaves would say, "O, pray, Marster! O, pray, Marster!"

When the slave was workin' good, they would sing like this:

> Watch the sun; see how she run;
> Never let her catch you with your work undone.
> Howdy, my brethern, howdy you do,
> Since I been in the land
> I do mighty well, and I thank the Lord, too,
> Since I been in the land
> O yes, O yes, since I been in the land
> O yes, O yes, since I been in the land
> I do mighty well, and I thank the Lord too,
> Since I been in the land.

There was another song that went sorta like this:

See my brother run down the hill
Fall down on he knees.
Send up your prayers;
I'll send up mine,
The good Lord to please.
Raise the heavens, high as the skies,
Fall down on your knees.
Send up your prayers;
I'll send up mine,
The good Lord to please.

When come quittin' time, them slaves would sing all the way to the house.

Marse Bill had plenty of ever'thing 'round him. He had a drove of cows and more milk than they knowed what to do with. He had hosses, mules, hogs, sheep, yard full of chickens, geese, guineas, peafowls, pigeons. He had two jennies and a jack, and he made big money off of them. He made plenty cotton, corn, rice, taters, and peas, and every good thing to eat. He planted more taters than anybody in the country. Them taters was red on the outside and white inside, and they would choke you if you didn't drink water with 'em. He made as many as fifty tater banks.

When he killed his hogs, he would smoke that meat and wrap it in shucks to keep it from spoilin'. That was better than you can buy right now.

He made his slaves pull fodder and stack it high. Then

he put some of it in the loft of the big barn. He had a rack in the lot and put that fodder in that rack, so his stock could eat it.

He made lots and lots of rice every year. Every Friday he made old Jim put some rice on a big cloth like a sheet and get switches and beat and beat that rice. Then old Jim would hold that rice high up and let it fall to the ground a little at a time. The wind would blow the chaff off, and then he had good rice left. That was the way he hulled his peas. He fed us on peas and rice.

Every Sat'day that come, Marse Bill would ration the slaves. He would call them up and give every family a little flour, rice, peas, meat, and meal, and sometimes a little soda. We had flour 'nough to make biscuits ever' Sunday mornin'. The rest of the time, they ate cornbread. If the rations give out 'fore next Sat'day— well, that was too bad, for you had to do without.

Let me tell you 'bout my uncle. He would get more whuppin's than anybody. He would steal. Marse Bill kept missin' meat out of the smokehouse, and he set up one night to catch the rogue. Well, 'bout midnight, Uncle Irwin prized up a log and took it out and crawled through that hole. Right there Marse Bill caught him, and what a whuppin' he did get. Then one time somebody was stealin' Marse Bill's corn, and Marse Bill set a trap to get that rogue. The next mornin', who was in the trap but Uncle Irwin! Well, he made Uncle Irwin dance over the place while he whupped him.

Uncle Irwin had to feed the hosses. You know, the chickens would lay eggs in the troughs, and every egg he would find would be his. Marse Bill used to catch him with the eggs oftentimes and whup him, but he would do that again. You couldn't put anything down, but Uncle Irwin would get it right now.

One time Marse Bill had a shote [shoat, or young, weaned pig] that stayed around the yard. Well, that shote come up missin' one day, and Marse Bill told young Marse Russ to fin' that shote. Well, Marse Russ found it where Uncle Irwin had killed it. Uncle Irwin had to dress that shote and put it in the smokehouse and take a whuppin' for it.

There was plenty milk on that place. They had the milk in a little house out under the chinaberry tree, close by the kitchen, but they kept that little milk house locked up all the time.

Marse Bill had a pet deer named Nan, and that deer was bad about buttin' all the chaps on the place. Every time I come close to that deer, she would butt me down, and I had to run. They told me not to run, but that deer got me for sho'.

Marse Bill would ride that big, black hoss all over the place. He was so black and slick he would shine. His bridle had martingale [the strap of a horse's harness passing from the noseband to the girth, between the fore-legs] on it, and that sho' was pretty. I just loved to see him ride that hoss.

Marse Bill had a big gin, called hosspower gin. You had to press the cotton with our feet and that was hard work.

I had to help my pappy shear the sheep. It was my job to catch the sheep and hold him while pappy done the cuttin'.

Marse Bill whupped me sometimes, and Mist'ess was all the time pullin' on my ears and slappin' me in the face, but the worse whuppin' I ever got was from my grandmammy—Viney, the cook. She cooked a tater pone and left it in the kitchen. After they left the kitchen, I slipped in there and got a big hunk of that tater pone. Well, Viney missed that hunk I got, and when grandmammy learnt I was the one that got it, she put the switch on and tore my back up salt crick. From that day 'til now I never eat a tater pone but I think 'bout that whuppin'.

We never had no lamps. The white folks had candles, and made them candles right on the place by meltin' tallow and pourin' it in molds. They made all the soap that they had by puttin' ashes in a hopper and pourin' water on 'em and takin' that water and boilin' it in a big pot with bone and old grease. That was good soap.

When the womens who had babies went to the field, they took them babies with them and made a pallet out of a old quilt in the fence corner and put them babies there while they hoed and plowed. Then some of the women had bigger chilluns that they would put there to watch the babies. When the babies would cry, and the mammies got to the end of the row, they would stop and nurse their babies. Then some of the big chaps had to tote water to the field for the hands—sometimes me and Tom had to tote water to them.

When it rained the women had to go to the loom house and work. They made all the jeans and Lowells and cloth right there and dyed some of it with copperas and maple bark. Them women could make pretty cloth. That cloth never wore out. In them days, the women wore hoops and what you call balmarals [Balmorals]— the white folks done it and so did the slave women.

The women had no combs, and my mammy comb her head with a cob, then wrap her hair and tie it up in a cloth. My mammy could tote a bucket of water on her head and never spill a drop. I seed her bring that milk in great big buckets from the pen on her head and never lose one drop.

I heard 'em talkin' 'bout the big fight [the Civil War] and sayin' they could whup 'em 'fore breakfast. After 'while, young Marse Russ was gone to help whup 'em, and then Marse Bill went 'way, too. All the time they was gone, the slaves kept prayin' to be set free. They would go down under the hill way in the night and pray hard to be set free.

One day I heard Viney hollerin', "The Yankees are comin'. The Yankees are comin'." And Tom and me run to the big house to see what the Yankees look like, and there they ridin' up the front lane, three abreast, all dressed in blue clothes—they sho' looked fine. They ride right over Mist'ess's flowers and tramped 'em down. Miss Hester was standin' on the front gallery, and one of them soldiers said, "We want a chunk of fire," and Mist'ess said, "You will have to get it from one of the darkies." Then the soldiers laughed. Then they said, "Have you got anything to eat?" and she said, "No," and then they broke the lock on the smokehouse door and poured all the 'lasses [molasses] out on the ground, and took all the meat and broke open that door and drunk all the milk, and what they did not drink they poured on the ground.

Some of them soldiers caught the chickens, and some of them had long knives like swords and rode their hosses right by the turkeys and reached down and cut off the head of every turkey. They took them turkeys and chickens down the lane and cooked 'em.

They went to the lot and took every hoss and left us some old scrubby stock that was worn out. Zias, one of the slaves, got on Marse Bill's pony named Daisy and went 'way with them Yankees. When he come back, he said they promised to give him forty acres of land and a mule, and all he got was a suit of blue clothes. He come home on foot 'cause they took his pony.

When them Yankees come up to the house, I was mighty scared. I got behind old granny's skirt and never let them see me. They went in the big house and took the new quilts and counterpins and put them under their saddles. They burnt the gin and all the cotton on the place and scattered all the corn out of the crib, and I had to help pick up what they left.

One mornin' just 'fore dinner, Marse Bill blowed that big horn and all the slaves come right to the big house. He told them that they was free now, but that he wanted them to stay with him 'til the crop was made, and he would pay them for it. Some of 'em left, but mammy and pappy stayed and I stayed with them.

After that Marse Bill didn't whip but he sho' did fuss. He got some more chickens, and sold the eggs, and bought plow tools, and they sold everything.

Marse Bill rationed out the food to the slaves, but he writ it down in a book and made the slave pay him for it at the end of the year. He promised to pay the slaves for their work, but when the end of the year come, the slaves owed him so much there was nothin' or mighty little comin' to 'em. The slaves had a hard time. All they made, the bossman took it, and iffen you moved to another plantation, you had to go with nothin'. The slaves had no hoss to plow, and the store man said he wouldn't sell 'em unless they had somethin' to make sure the store man was goin' to get his money. We had no 'lasses or taters. We had nothin'.

I was getting to be a big youngster. After I stayed there with Marse Bill a few years, I left there and went up the country and hired to Mr. Addison Burris. He fed me and give me fifty cent a day. I made some money that year. After 'while I married and settled down. One year I said to Mr. Burris, "I want to borrow some money from you." He said, "How much do you want?" He said, "Well, if I let you have that much you will have to pay me fifteen percent intrust [interest]." I said, "I'll do that." He got a little black box and counted that money out to me. That was the most money I ever seed in my life at one time. I took that money and bought me a hoss and wagon and something to eat for the year. That year I made twelve bales of cotton and 'bout four hundred barrels of corn. I never done that well any more. That was the best year in my life.

My first wife is dead. We had three chilluns. Then I married Mary Davis. She lived in Summit. We had no chilluns. I am a Baptist and belong to the Collins Grove Baptist Church near Summit. I is old now and own my little home. One of my grandsons live with us, but I tries to help 'round the place some.

I's seen some mighty hard times. I remember after the war my mammy would roast corncobs and take the inside out of it and use that soda. It would make the bread rise jus' like soda. We parched tater peelin' and made coffee. We dug up the dirt in the smokehouse and dripped that through the hopper and biled [boiled] that to get salt.

After we work for the white man all our lives and then when we was set free, he never give the slaves anything. Some of the old-timers would steal, but I never stole anything after that tater pone whuppin'.

One time the white caps [Ku Klux Klan] came to my house and ask for me. I sure was scared. My wife told them that I was not there, and they just told her to tell me I musn't work for a certain man 'cross the crick, and I couldn't trade with the Jews anymore. Well, I was hid up in the loft of the house and heard every word they said. They didn't bother me.

My grandpappy could hoodoo anybody. He had a long string of beads and could say prayers over 'em. Then he could brew a tea and put one of them beads in it and tell you that would cure rummatiz [rheumatism]. When you would drink that, you would sho' do some devilment or go crazy-like. Yo' eyesight would get bad, and you would have pains in yo' head and feel like you was goin' to die.

One time I seed him make a nigger spit cotton after he had drunk a cup of his tea. Ever'body said he was a bad nigger. He never could hoodoo me. I would get out of his way. I was too smart for him.

Nettie Henry

Age 82 when interviewed
at her home in Meridian, Mississippi

The Chil's place was at Livingston, Alabama, on Alamucha Creek. That's where I was born, but I just did get borned good when Miss Lizzie—she was Marse Chil's girl—married Marse John C. Higgins and moved to Meridian. Me and my mammy and my two sisters, Liza and Tempe, was give to Miss Lizzie.

I ain't no country nigger. I was raised in town. My mammy cooked and washed and ironed and done ever'thing for Miss Lizzie. She live right where Miss Annie—she was Miss Lizzie's daughter—live now. But then the house face Eighth Street 'stead of Seventh Street, like it do now. They warn't any other houses in that block. Before the Surrender, they turned the house to face Seventh Street 'cause the town was growin' and a heap of folks was buildin' houses. I tell you somethin' 'bout Seventh Street in a minute. Couldn't nobody that lived in Meridian right after the Surrender ever forget Seventh Street and where it head to.

My pappy didn' go with us to Meridian. He belonged to one set of white people, you see, and my mammy belonged to another. He'd come to see us 'til the war started, then his folks just kinda went to Texas. I don't know why exactly 'cept maybe it warn't so healthy for 'em 'round Livingston. They didn't go to the war or nothin'. I 'spect nice white folks talked 'bout 'em and wouldn't have nothin' to do with 'em. So they took and went to Texas and took my pappy with 'em. But after the war he come back to us, walked 'most all the way from Texas. He rented some land from Mr. Ragsdale. My pappy built us a shack on that land. It's tore down now, but it was built good. Us all helped. I pulled a cross-cut saw and toted the boards up the roof on a ladder. The chimley was built out of mud and rocks. Then us moved in and started growin' us somethin' to eat. Us didn't have no horse and plow. Yankees done carried off all the horses and mules and burnt up ever'thing, like plows. Us dug up the ground with a grubbin' hoe and raised punkins and plenty of chickens and ever'thing.

Us lived nice. My people was smart. My white

people was good white people. They warn't brutish; never whupped us or nothin' like that. I don' know nothin' 'bout no meanness.

Mr. Higgins, he died pretty soon, and Miss Lizzie went to teachin' school. Her chillun—Miss Annie and them—would try to teach us. Then us carried Blue Back Spellers to Sunday school, and a old Baptist colored preacher would teach us out of it. He say, "The same words is in this book what's in the Bible. You chillun learn 'em the way they is fixed for you to learn 'em in this here Blue Black Speller, then the first thing you know you can read the Bible." Us went to the white folks' church durin' the war and right after. Any of the white folks can tell you 'bout Mr. Preacher Hamlin. He was a preacher and a schoolteacher mixed. He had the first boardin' school for young white ladies. It's standin' right there on Eighth Street right now. I 'members the first one to gragurate [graduate] from it. Well, Mr. Hamlin 'nitiated my pappy right there in the white folks' church, the First Baptist Church. It burn up long time ago. My pappy was Isam Allbrook. He was the first colored deacon ordained in Meridian.

I was ten years old at the surrender, but I took notice. Them was scary times, and when you is scared you take trigger-notice. It was next to the last year of the war 'fore Sherman got to Meridian—not Sherman hisself but soldiers. They burnt up that big house on Eighth Street hill and built camps for the soldiers in the flower garden. The captains went and lived in Marse Greer's house. Marse Greer done sunk all the silver in the duck pond and hid out the horses and cows in the big canebrake what used to be on this side of Sowashee Creek. But, Lord, it didn't do no good. Sherman done caught on by that time 'bout how to find things. They got ever'thing and burned Marse Greer's barn. They left the house and didn't bother the family 'cause they called theyselfs company. The good Lord knows Marse Greer didn't 'vite 'em! But the captain's bein' there kept the rip-rap [riff-raff] soldiers from tearin' up ever'thing.

When word come that they was comin', it sound like a moanin' wind in the quarter. Ever'body was a-sayin', "The Yankees is comin'! The Yankees is comin'!" Us chillun was scared, but it was like Sunday, too—nobody doin' nothin'. Us march 'round the room and sorter sing-like, "The Yankees is comin'! The Yankees is comin'!" They wouldn't let us out in the big road. Well, they come. They burn up seventy houses and all the stores. They tore up the railroad tracks and toted off ever'thing they couldn't eat. I don't understand nothin' 'bout how come they act like that. Us ain't done nothin' to 'em.

Well, things kept gettin' worse and worse. After the Surrender, niggers got might biggity. Most of 'em was glad just to feel free. They didn' have no better sense. They forgot wouldn't be nobody to take care of 'em. Things warn't healthy, and my mammy and me kept close to the white folks. Course, Tempe, she was grown and could do what she please. She sho' done somethin' when she married Cal. That was the meanest nigger! He nail up a board over the gatepost what say, "No visitors allowed." Sure-'nough didn't no visitors want to go to his house!

I don't know how come things got so unnat'ral after the Surrender. Niggers got to bein' all kind of things what the Lawd didn't intend 'em for, like bein' policemen and all like that. It was scand'lous! Course it was the Yankees what done it. They promise to give ever'body forty acres land and a mule. A lot of 'em didn't have no better sense than to believe 'em. They'd go 'head and do what the Yankees would tell 'em. Well, they didn't give 'em nothin', not even a rooster. Didn't give 'em nothin' but trouble.

I don't know how come Mr. Theodore Sturges's brother was a Yankee. But after the Surrender, he come to Meridian and got to be mayor. Didn't none of the white folks like that. Mr. Theodore didn't like it hisself, but nothin' he could do 'bout it. Things got so bad the Klu Kluxes started ridin' at night and 'sposin' [disposing] of bad niggers. Then one Sat'day night, Mr. Theodore's big store got set fire to and the mayor tried to blame it on the Klu Kluxes. Course ever'body knowed the Yankees done it. You see the Yankees was a-tryin' to get the gov'nor to run the Klu Kluxes out. That was one awful fire. Near 'bout the whole town burnt up downtown, and every nice white man was down there a-fightin' the fire.

Plenty o' niggers was out, too, doin' devilishment. Three of 'em got arrested, and they had the trial Monday. In the meantime, all the Yankee-lovin' niggers had a big meetin', and the loudest mouth there was that big buck Nigger Bill. Here they [the blacks] goes, all het [heated] up from makin' speeches and a-drinkin', and pack the courtroom full. When Mr. Patton got up on the stand, Bill holler out, "That's a lie!" Then Mr. Patton raise up his walkin' stick and start toward Bill. 'Bout then Bill jerk out his pistol and shoot at Mr. Patton. He miss Mr. Patton and hit Judge Bremlette, kill him corpse-dead right there on his high pulpit chair!

'Bout that time ever'thing bust loose. Near 'bout all the white gentlemen in the courtroom take a shot at Bill. He falls, but he ain't dead yet. They put him in the sheriff's office and left two white men with him. But things was a-happenin' so fast by that time they couldn't stand it. They throwed Bill out of that two-story window and run down to get in the fight. The white folks was plumb wore out by that time with all the devilishment of the Yankees and the fool niggers. Even a mean nigger got sense 'nough to know when he done gone too far. They all get away as fast as they could and scatter over town, then after dark they come a-creepin' back to the quarters. That was sho' the wrong thing to do. That night, all the sure-'nough white men come a-marchin' out Seventh Street on they way to the quarters.

I had did up Miss Lizzie's parlor curtains that very day, and the boy was puttin' up the moldin' frame 'round 'em when us hear that trompin' sound. It didn't sound like no ever'day marchin'. It sound like Judgment Day. The boy fell off the ladder and run and hide behind the flour barrel in the pantry. Miss Lizzie was peepin' out 'tween them white lace curtains, and I was right behind her. I 'spect Seventh Street was lined with womenfolk doin' just what us doin', 'cause they husbands, sons, and sweethearts was out there in that march line.

Well, that night ended all the troubles. The line done stop at Mr. Theodore Sturges's house 'fore it get out far as us. Course, ever'body know Mr. Theodore and Miss Allie was sure-'nough folks, but they was bound to have that Yankee brother of his.

The yard was plumb full of white men ready to burn the house right down on Miss Allie's head lessen they give up that Yankee mayor. Mr. Theodore come to the door and say, "Gentlemen, he ain't here." Ain't nobody believe that. They was a-fixin' to busy on in anyhow, when Miss Allie come out. She come right down them steps 'mongst all them mad folks and say, calm and ladylike, "Gentlemen, my brother-in-law is here, certainly. Where would he go for safety 'cept to his brother's house? But I give you my word, he goin' to stay right here 'til you put him on the first train headin' North. Then no mo' blood will be spilled." And that's what they done.

It was all might bad, but plenty good things done happen in Meridian, too. I's seen this town grow from nothin'. When us come here 'fore the war, they was hitchin' they horses to little oak bushes right in the middle o' town where the biggest stores is now. I was a grown girl by then and could make horsemint tea for chills and mullein leaves for fever good as anybody; and horehound tea for colds, bitter as gall.

I married when I was nineteen years old. I had nine chilluns and five of 'em is still livin'. They looks after me right nice, too. My son in Chicago gimme this house, and I lives here by myself. I keeps it nice and clean. I tries to live like a Christian and do just like Old Mist'ess say. Then when I die, I can go to Heaven.

Susan Snow

Age 87 when interviewed
at her home in Meridian, Mississippi

I was born in Wilcox County, Alabama, in 1850. W.J. Snow was my old marster. He bought my ma from a man named Jerry Casey. Venus was her name, but they mostly call her "Venie."

I's workin' now for one of my old folks. I can't work much—just carries things to her and such. She's my old mist'ess's own daughter, and she's got grandchillun grown and married.

When her [Snow's current employer] bought my pappy, I was a baby. Her pa owned a heap of niggers. I's the only one still hangin' around.

My ma was a black African, and she sho' was wild and mean. She was so mean to me I couldn't believe she was my mammy. They couldn't whip her without tyin' her up first. Sometimes my marster would wait 'til the next day to get somebody to help tie her up, then he'd forget to whip her. They used to say she was a conger [conjure] woman, and they was all scared of her. But my ma was scared of congers, too.

All the niggers on the place was born in the family and was kin 'cept my ma. She told me how they brought her from Africa. You know, like we say "president" in this country, well, they call him "chief" in Africa. Seem like the chief made 'rangements with some men and they had a big goober grabbin' for the young folks. They stole my ma and some more and brung 'em to this country.

I don't 'member nothin' 'bout havin' no pa. In them days, husbands and wives didn't belong to the same folks. My ma say her husband was so mean that after us left Alabama she didn't want to marry no more.

A man didn't get to see his wife 'cept twice a week. That was Wednesday and Sat'day night.

The women had to walk a chalkline [stay faithful to their husbands]. I never heard tell of wives runnin' 'round with other men in them days.

I was raised in Jasper County. Marster bought land from ever'body 'round 'til he had a big plantation. He had niggers, horses, mules, cows, hogs, and chickens. He was a rich man then.

Every nigger had a house of his own. My ma never would have no board floor like the rest of 'em, on 'count she was a African—only dirt. They say she was 108 year old when she died.

Us went to church with the white folks if us wanted to. They didn't make us. I didn't go much, 'cause I didn't have 'ligion then. Us didn't have no schoolin'. Us could go to school with the white chillun if us wanted to, but didn't nobody teach us. I's educated, but I ain't educated in the books. I's educated in the licks and lumps I got.

My white folks was good people and didn't whip nobody 'less they needed it. Some of the niggers was sure-'nough bad. They used to take the marster's horses out at night and ride 'em down. One nigger, Sam, got that mad at a mule for grabbin' at cotton, he cut his tongue out. Course, Marster whipped him, but when he went to look for him 'bout a hour after, he found him sound asleep. Said he ought to kill him, but he didn't.

When we was sick, they had a doctor for us just like they done for theyselves. They called him in to 'scribe [prescribe medicine] for us. I was snakebit when I was eight years old. They used to be a medicine, "lobelia." The doctor give me that and whiskey. My ma carried me up to the big house every mornin' and left me, and carried me home at night. Old Miss would watch over me in the daytime.

My young marster told me that when I got to be ten year old, I'd have a snake coiled up on my liver.

That scared me most to death 'til I was past ten year old.

They made all the niggers' clothes on the place. Homespun they called it. They had spinnin' wheels and cards and looms at the big house. All the women spinned in the wintertime.

I never knowed what it was to wear more than one garment 'til I was 'most grown. I never had a pair of shoes of my own. Old Miss let me wear hers sometimes. They had shoes for the old folks, but not for the chillun.

I got more whippin's than any other nigger on the place, 'cause I was mean like my mammy. Always a-fightin' and scratchin' with white and black. I was so bad Marster made me go look at the niggers they hung to see what they done to niggers that harm a white man.

I's going to tell this story on myself. The white chillun where a-singin' this song:

Jeff Davis, long and slim
whipped old Abe with a hickory limb.

Jeff Davis is a wise man, Lincoln is a fool.
Jeff Davis rides a gray, and Lincoln rides a mule.

I was mad anyway, so I hopped up and sung this one:

Old Gen'ral Pople had a shotgun,
Filled it full of gum,

Killed 'em as they come.

Called a Union band,
Make the Rebels understand,
To leave the land,
Submit to Abraham.

Old Miss was a-standin' right behind me. She grabbed up the broom and laid it on me. She made me submit. I caught the feathers, don't you forget it.

I didn't know it was wrong. I'd heard the niggers sing it, and I didn't know they was a-singin' in they sleeves. I didn't know nothin' 'bout Abe Lincoln, but I heard he was a-tryin' to free the niggers, and my mammy say she want to be free.

The young folks used to make up a heap of songs then. They'd decompose [compose] they own songs and sing 'em. I never will forget one song they sung when they buried anybody. It made Old Marster, Mist'ess, and all of 'em cry. Us chillun cried, too. It went like this:

My mother prayed in the wilderness,
In the wilderness,
In the wilderness.
My mother prayed in the wilderness.
And then I'm a-goin' home.

Then I'm a-goin' home,

Then I'm a-goin' home.

We'll all make ready, Lord,
And then I'm a goin' home.

She plead her cause in the wilderness,
In the wilderness,
In the wilderness.
She plead her cause in the wilderness.
And then I'm a-goin' home.

Old Aunt Hannah fell to my marster from his daddy. She had twelve chillun a-workin' on the place. The oldest was named Adam, and the littlest was named Eve. She had two twins what was named Rachel and Leah. They nursed Mist'ess's two twins. They kept one a-nursin' most all the time.

My ma was the cause of my marster a-firin' all the overseers. They blamed ever'thing on her 'cause she was the only bought nigger. Marster say she was a valuable nigger, but she was so mean he was afraid they'd kill her. He say, "She'll work without no watchin' and overseers ain't nothin', nohow."

They was a white man—I ain't lyin'—I know him, and I seen him. He had nigger hounds, and he made money a-huntin' runaway niggers. His own niggers killed him. They hung 'em for it. Two was his niggers, and one belong to somebody else.

My young marster used to work in the field with

us. He'd boss the niggers. They called him Bud, but us all called him "Babe." I sho' did love that boy.

When the war come, they used to tease him and say, "Bud, why don't you go to the war?" They laughed and teased him when he went. But warn't no laughin' when he come home on a furlough and went back. They was a-cryin' then. And well they might cry, 'cause he never come back no more. He was killed in the war.

Durin' the war, the white folks made they clothes same as the niggers. Old Miss made dye and dyed thread. She made pretty cloth.

My ma was the first to leave the plantation after the Surrender. All the other niggers had a contract to stay, but she didn't. She went to Newton County and hired out. She never wanted to stay in one place, nohow. If she had a crop half made and somebody made her mad, she'd up and leave it and go somewhere else.

You know, they was might strict 'bout then with colored folks and white people, too. The Klu Kluxes was out nights. I heard tell 'bout 'em whippin' people. But they never bothered me.

They was speakers goin' aroun', tellin' the niggers what they was going to get. They never got nothin' to my knowledge, 'cept the gov'ment let 'em homestead land. My ma homesteaded a place close to Enterprise, Scott County, but she got mad and left it like she always done.

She was a-gettin' 'long in years 'fore she got religion.

She was good to me after that. She couldn't learn the Lord's Prayer, but she used to pray, "Our Father, which are in heaven, hallowed be Thy name. Thy mercy, Lord, you've showed to others, that mercy show to me. Amen." She went to rest in it, too.

I went to Enterprise, then to Meridian, nursin', wet nursin' when I could, and workin' out. I never worked in the field, if I could help it. Old Miss hired me out as a nurse first when I was eight year old.

When I come to Meridian, I cut loose. I's tellin' the truth! I's a woman, but I's a prodigal. I used to be a old drunkard. My white folks kept tellin' me if I got locked up one more time, they wouldn't pay my fine. But they done it again and again.

The niggers called me "Devil." I was a devil 'til I got religion. I warn't baptized until 1887. Then I found peace. I had a vision. I told it to a white lady, and she say, "Susie, that's religion a-callin' you." But you know, honey, white folks' religion ain't like niggers' religion. I know a woman that couldn't 'member the Lord's Prayer, and she got religion outa prayin', "January, February, March!" I didn't join the church 'til 1891, after I had a second vision. I's a member in good standin' now. I done put all my badness behind me, 'cept my temper. I even got that under more control.

I didn't used to be scared of conjures. I's scared now, 'cause I had it done to me. I went to bed well and healthy, and the next mornin' I couldn't get up at all.

I's tellin' the truth. A colored man done it. He was a crippled man and mean as he could be. I was good to him, too. He told me 'bout it hisself.

He went to the graveyard and got some o' the meanest dirt he could find (I don't know how he knowed which was the meanest grave) and put it under my doorsill. He sho' fix me. I ask him how come he done it to me, and I been so good to him. He smile kinda tickle-like and say, "It's a good thing you was good to me, 'cause, if you hadn't of been you'd be dead in yo' grave by now."

I ain't got nary a soul what's kin to me that I knows of. I don't want none of 'em comin' to me now and a-sayin', "Don't you 'member yo' own cousin?" My white folks help me when I needs it.

These young folks. Shucks! They worse'n what I was, only they's more slyer. That's all.

I's glad I's got religion, 'cause when I dies, I's going to the "Good Place."

Frank Williams

Age 85 when interviewed
in Monroe County, Mississippi

I's not exactly sho' how old I is right to the day, but
Miss Ellie write to Miss Mary, one of my mistress's
chillun, and she say I was 'bout two months older than
her and that'd throw me bein' born 'bout the first part
of December in 1852. My mammy and daddy was name
Elvira and Henry Williams, and they come to Pontotoc,
where my mammy say I was born, from Virginny. 'Fore
I was big enough to know it, we moved to Marse
Conoway's (he was the man who first bought my folks)
place that was about sixteen miles from Aberdeen, up
towards Nettleton. When I was 'bout five years old,
Marse Conoway give us to his daughter, Miss Martha.
She had done runned off with his overseer, Tom

Williams, and married him, and him with no mo' than the clothes he had on his back. Marse Conoway love her though and was good to her and give them a farm and a passel of his niggers.

Tom Williams was a sorta mean man and right hard to get along with. He never was a rich man either, even after the good farm what the ole marster give him. We didn't live in no quarters like they did on the big plantation but just had our little houses scattered over the place. We had plenty to eat, but that was all.

I had nine brothers and sisters and all of them 'cept me and my brother next to me worked in the field all day. They didn't send me 'cause I was too little and didn't send my brother 'cause he looked like he was going to be such a big hefty man that they didn't want to stunt his growth any. It didn't make much difference how smart a nigger was when a man went to sell him if he was big and strong, and Tom Williams thought he sell him for a big price when he get grown.

I worked 'round the lot and drove the mules and cows and fanned the flies off Miss Martha when she was sick. I helped 'round the still, too, where Marse Tom made his likker. There was a long trough where it run off when it was made, and me and my brother would drink all we could hold when he warn't lookin'. We'd get powerful drunk and have a big time. We made whiskey, yeller peach brandy, apple jack, and everything. He like his likker, Tom Williams did. He had a peach orchard and apple orchard that he never used for nothin' else. Even as chillun we could get all we wanted to drink, but if he caught us, he'd tie our hands together and put them over our heads and whip us. He'd do that to all the niggers when they didn't do to suit him. But he never whipped us chillun so hard, and the most fun that we had in them days was stealin' whiskey, drinkin' it, and fightin'.

We didn' have no church on our little place then, and I don't 'member anything 'bout my folks goin' off the place to no meetin's. Once in a while they went to the white folks' church and sit in the back or on the outsides. We never had no kinda school either. Why, even our marster couldn't read or write, but Miss Martha could. And they had a passel of chillun, and she taught them.

I sho' 'members the war. The soldiers march past our place all the time. I mean our soldiers, not the Yankees. They would bring they hosses what was broken down and hide 'em in our pasture 'til they get well. Then they would come and get them. They always left a soldier behind to keep an eye on them, but we'd have to see that they got tended to. Tom Williams got him many a good hoss out of them that was put there in our pasture. He didn't go to the war until it was 'most over. Miss Martha died while he was away. We sho' did hate that 'cause we really belonged to her and not to him.

One of Miss Martha's girls married purty soon after that. She married one of the soldiers that camped on the place. After the war, she went to Texas with him.

After the war and Tom Williams had come home, he call ever'body together and tell them they was free but that he want to hire them 'til Christmas—that was in May—to help lay the crop. He said he'd pay good wages, too. Ever'body stayed, but the next spring my daddy say he going to leave. Now I guess he was one of the biggest niggers anywhere 'round, and he was right smart, too. He could run a gin and was a right pert carpenter. Tom Williams wanted him to stay, but my daddy didn't have much use for him. So he say he going to leave anyhow. Then Tom Williams got mad and grabbed my daddy's hands and tied them over his head to a branch on a oak tree and holler to me, "By the Lord God who made Moses, go get my whip, Frank!" He took the whip what was made out of a gin belt and lashed my daddy 'til the blood come. He say, "Now, you change yo' mind and give up?" and my daddy still say no. He left him there three or four days, but all the time he made me stay with him and bring him water and bread. Then he thought he might die, so's he say, "Henry, I's going to let you down and give you a nice soft bed on the porch 'til you makes up your mind." But 'fore he unties his hands, he put a chain on his legs. Then he carries him over to the porch and chains him to one of the posts. He say, "Henry, I'm going to let you have one of Miss Martha's soft beds, and I'm going to feed you fried chicken. Now, is you going to stay?"

He kept him there for about a week, but my daddy

never did say he would stay. Finally Tom Williams go out and tell ever'body for miles around that my daddy is a bad nigger, and that he wouldn't work, and for none of them to hire him. Then he come home and tell daddy what he done and turn him loose and say, "Now, go get a job, if you can." He thought all the time my daddy would have to come back to him so's his family wouldn't starve to death. We set out and come to Aberdeen, and all of us worked hard at one thing and then another. I was houseboy in two or three places. My daddy worked a little farm and made horse collars to sell. We finally save up enough to buy that little farm.

It warn't long after that when I went to work on a gov'ment boat on the river. We cleaned out the Tombigbee River, on up to Towne Creek, near where we first lived. I worked there for 'bout four years.

I's married to the third wife now. We haven't got but three chillun livin'. Our girl lives in Amory, and our two boys in Chicago. One of them's a barber and doin' right well. The other is right smart, too.

Course I's glad slavery's over. We always had plenty to eat, and I didn't have such a hard time. But I ain't going to never forget 'bout my daddy bein' 'most whipped to death. After I had growed up, I 'spect I would have got the same treatment. The white folks I's knowed since then, though, has been good to me, and I thinks a lot of them. But I's glad those other days is over.

Rina Brown

Age 84 when interviewed
at her home in McComb, Mississippi

I was eighty-four years old this past June gone by, and I was a big gal when the war closed, and we was set free.

I was born in Franklin County on the Homochitto River, on the east side, 'bout forty-five miles from Natchez. There is a settlement at that place now named Monroe, Mississippi. I lived in that neighborhood all my life 'til nineteen hundred and 'leven, when I come to McComb to live with my daughter.

My marse was John F. Lea, and my mistess was Miss Atlanta Lea. They was the best white folks that ever lived on this earth. I was raised right in the house and nursed Miss Atlanta's two boys. I ate at the kitchen table and had all the things to eat the white folks had to eat. I slept on a little bed in the corner of the back room.

My mist'ess whupped me when I needed it, but she was always good to me and give me nice clothes to wear.

We had a big eight-room house, but it was all on the ground floor. The kitchen was in the backyard, whilst the dining room was in the big house. I helped tote the grub from the kitchen to the dining room. It was my job to tote the dishes back to be washed.

We had no well and had to tote the water from the spring, and it was down the hill. Every time Miss Atlanta wanted to take a bath, I had to put a big washtub in the back room, and then go down to the spring and tote the water up that hill and pour it in the tub, so she could take her bath. They didn't know what a bathtub in the house was.

They had no carpets or rugs on the floors. Every time they wanted the floor scrubbed, I had to tote water from the spring. My mammy did the scrubbin'. She had a mop made with holes bored in it and shucks pulled through it. She put sand and home-made soap on that floor and pull that mop over it. When she rinsed it off, that floor sho' was white and clean.

My mammy was named Liddy, and she was the cook. She done the washin' and ironin,' and she cleaned the house, and she milked, too. She used to take clothes down to the spring and wash, and made me go down there and battle the clothes. There was no washboards in them days, and she used homemade soap.

Every year after hog-killin' time, my mammy would drip lye through the ash hopper and make a barrel of soap. That soap would get the dirt outen them clothes.

The slave quarters was 'bout half-mile from the big house, 'cross the crick, but my mammy lived right in the backyard. She helped do all the work 'round the place. Mr. Lea had no overseer, so he made my pappy a kinda straw boss over the work hands.

My pappy was named Wilson Lea. He drove the team to market, and fed the hosses and pigs, and plowed the garden, and work in the field like the rest of the slaves.

There was a house over in the quarters where Granny stayed and kept the chaps while their mammies was in the field. Granny lived to be one hundred and fifteen years old, and she tended to the little chaps. Granny smoked a pipe and kept her head tied up in a red-flowered hank'chief.

Granny's name was Nanny, and she was my pappy's mammy. She said she come with the older Leas to this country way back yonder when there was just a few colored people in Mississippi, and this country was full of Injuns, and they was ready to fight.

She said when they first come here they had no plows and made the crops with just a hoe. One year she made a bale of cotton and a load of corn with her hoe. Them days there was no gins 'round there. They picked up the lint from the seed with their hands and then carded that lint, spun it, made thread of it, and then made the cloth. After a while, they put that cotton in bags and sent it to Natchez and had it put in bales. She said they put corn in a wooden bowl and pestled it 'til it was fine 'nough to make bread. Her marse was named Joseph Lea.

After Marse Joseph Lea died, his wife married a Mr. Grissum, and my mammy fell heir to [was inherited by] her son by her first husband, John F. Lea. My pappy belonged to Mr. Grissum, and Marse John Lea bought him. My mammy had ten chilluns, but only four lived. They was Rose, Chaney, Rina, and Prustess. All of them is dead 'cept me.

While workin' round the house, I heard them talkin' 'bout folks buildin' the railroad from New Orleans to Summit. Every time anybody would pass that way, Marse always asked them "How far they got with the railroad?"

Then I heard them talk 'bout the big war and how the South could whup them Yankees. After 'while Marse John went off to the war. He was not gone many months 'fore he come back and said he was sick with the consumption. He was on the bed a long time and died. My pappy stayed right by his bed and tended to him all the time he was sick.

He had a big funeral, and all the white folks for miles 'round, and some of the black folks, too, come to see him buried.

He died in the fall of the year, and the next spring my mist'ess married again. This time his name was Mr. Moulter. He was right kind to the slaves and was there when we was set free.

The Yankees never come to our house, but I heard them talking 'bout how the Yankees went to some plantations and destroyed ever'thing. I never seed a Yankee, but some of the Southern soldiers would drop in and ask for somethin' to eat. Mist'ess would give them the best she had. Some of them soldiers was on their way home on a furlough. My mist'ess never refuse to feed them soldiers.

I remember when they fought the battle at Vicksburg. We could hear the cannons roar and then the glass in the windows would shake and rattle like a earthquake was comin'. Them was awful times.

All the slaves wanted to be set free so they could do like they please with no boss over them. They wanted to go places and have no patteroller catch them. Then they wanted to make money like the white folks and do their own buyin'.

One mornin' Mr. Moulter told all the slaves they was free now. He stood on the back steps and read the papers to them. Then he asked them to stay on the place and finish the crop—they all agreed to stay. They work mighty hard and got nothin' for it, so the next year they went somewhere else to work.

My mammy stayed with Miss Atlanta that year. The

next year she went to Mr. Pink Harrington and took her chaps with her. We all work mighty hard and when the end of the year come, we got nothin'. That is the way it always was—we work hard and get nothin' for it.

When we left Miss Atlanta's she give us nothin' to take with us. Ever'thing we got we had to buy on a credit, and then the white man got what we made. Times was mighty hard after the war—nearly starvation. My mammy was a good washer and ironer, and she went from house to house and done the fine clothes for the white ladies. They paid her in old clothes and a little somethin' to eat.

I married while I was young. No, we had no preacher to marry us. We just took up together. He just lived a short time, then I married Wash Brown. He is the pappy of all my chilluns. We had twelve. Some of them is dead, and my two oldest gals went to the Delta years ago. I ain't heard from them in more than two years. I's got seven chaps livin' right here in McComb. I stay with them, and they do the best they can for me.

I stayed right in the same neighborhood all my life, near where I was born, 'til nineteen hundred and 'leven, when my husband died. 'Fore he died, he told me to go to McComb and let the gals take care of me so long as I live.

When I got to McComb, the railroad was havin' a big strike in the shops. They was shootin' up trains, and put the men to work behind a big wall. Them was scary times for a country Negro.

The white folks and the colored folk used to have big dances, and old Joe would play the fiddle while they stepped lightly all the fancy steps. Just 'fore they would break up in morning, they would dance the Old Virginia Reel and then sing:

> Run, nigger, run, the patteroller'll get you.
> Run, nigger, run, it's almost day.
> That nigger run, that nigger flew
> That nigger lost his brogan shoe.
> Run, nigger, run, it's almost day.

Another song they used to sing and dance was:

> Come 'long gals and let's go to Boston,
> Come 'long gals and let's go to Boston,
> Come 'long gals and let's go to Boston,
> Early in the mornin'.
> Jack, Jack, Jack, I'll tell yo' daddy,
> Jack, Jack, Jack, I'll tell yo' daddy,
> Jack, Jack, Jack, I'll tell yo' daddy,
> Where you go a-courtin'.
> Reckon I care if you tell my daddy,
> Reckon I care if you tell my daddy,
> Reckon I care if you tell my daddy,
> Where I go a courtin'.

Them was good, and ever'body liked it. Some of them menfolks would get a little too much to drink, but they never done no mischief.

Miss Atlanta didn't have a loom house. She made the women card the cotton and spin the thread and sent it over to her mammy's and have it made into cloth. That cloth was brought home and made into fine clothes. Them days the ladies wore wide skirts and wide petticoats. The petticoats had ruffle after ruffle on them and made the dresses stand way out yonder. Then they wore hoop skirts, and when they walk with them long dresses on they had to lift them skirts in the front. Then after that they used to wear bustles behind to make them skirts stand out in the back. They wore lace capes round their shoulders and pretty little bonnets on their heads. Miss Atlanta had a little feather on the side of her bonnet. She wore gloves that had no fingers in them.

Marse John and Mist'ess never had a carriage, but ever'where they went they rode horseback. Mist'ess would set up straight as an arrow on that hoss. She rode a sidesaddle and a long skirt that almost touched the ground. Marse John always had spurs on his feet when he would ride. When he would get off that hoss, you could hear them spurs clack and make a big fuss.

Well, Mist'ess's husband died, and she married again. This time his name was Montgomery, but she didn't live long after she married this last time. She just had two boys, and I helped her raise them. They was name William and Muggins. They are all dead now.

After I come to McComb, I washed a little and done what little work I could to help make a livin'. Fourteen years ago, I was piecing quilts scraps when I seed my eyesight was failin' me. My sight kept on gettin' dimmer and worser and I went stone blind. I ain't seed daylight now for fourteen years. All I can do is to set here and wait for the good Lord to come and claim me for his own.

I study all the time 'bout my heavenly home. I know my time is most 'spired [expired] and I am livin' and prayin' to know right from wrong. If my chaps go 'stray, it's their own responsibility.

People nowadays do not recognize the house of the Lord. That is one house that ever'body should honor. When I carried my chaps to church, I would set them down on the bench or the floor. Iffen I had to serve the table, my chaps knowed better than to holler out in the Lord's house. Now when I go to church, I can't hear the preacher preach for so much racket going on 'twixt the mothers and the chaps. 'Pears to me they got no respect for the Lord's house.

I is a Methodist. I used to be a shoutin' Methodist, but now I is a missionary Methodist. I can't go to church often 'cause we have to hire a car to take me and that cost money, but bless the Lord, I can pray at home, and He hears my prayer.

Barney Alford

Age unknown when interviewed
at his home in Pike County, Mississippi

Marse Edwin Alford owned a big plantation right near the Louisiana state line. He had many slaves. I was borned on that place on what was called the State Line Road, in a little log house right back of the kitchen and not far from the chicken house.

My mammy was the cook for the ole missus. Another ole woman named Lit lived in one corner of the yard. She took care of all the black chilluns, and I played 'round her door steps 'til I was a big fellow. They said I was mighty bad 'cause I was always into mischief.

Marse Edwin had a big man for overseer, and that man whipped me every day. I would run the chickens offen the nest and let the cows and calves together. One time I tied a bundle of fodder to the tail of a horse and was 'bout to set it on fire when the overseer caught me. Then he sho' whipped me hard. Most of the time he would whip me with his hand. Sometimes he used a rope. But he had a post he tied the grown ones to and whipped them with a big whip. He was a hard man on the slaves.

Ole Missus was the best woman in the world, and ole Marster was good when he was not mad. But when you made him mad, he would have you whipped. He believed in makin' you work, and if you done your work right that would please him. If you would not work like he said, he just made you do it, and then the overseer laid it on you.

Ole Marse saw to it that we all had plenty to eat. Every Sat'day he give every family their portion to last for a week. And then, all of the niggers had their gardens and 'tato patch 'round their home.

No nigger could leave that place without a piece of paper with ole Marse's name on it. That was to keep the patteroller from gettin' him. But some of the niggers would slip off and go to the next-door plantation to see other slaves. They always went at night, when the white folks was asleep, and sometime they was caught.

Marse Alford had his daddy with him a whole lot of the time. The old man said he was borned in North Carolina and come here when the gov'ment was givin' 'way land. There was nothin' here but woods then.

I was borned in that little house back of the kitchen, and I lived there 'til after the Surrender. I's don't know what year I was borned, but they told me I was twelve years old when I was freed. My mammy had seven chilluns, and I was the firstborn. The first thing I remember was helpin' to tend other chilluns.

Ole Mammy Lit was mighty old. She lived in one corner of the big yard, and she cared for all the black chilluns while the old folks work in the field. Mammy Lit was good to all the chilluns, and I had to help her with them chilluns and keep them babies on the pallet. Mammy Lit smoked a pipe, and sometimes I would hide that pipe, and she would slap me for it. Then sometimes I would run 'way and go to the kitchen where my mammy was at work, and Mammy Lit would have to come for me. Then she would whip me again. She said I was bad.

The overseer whipped me nearly every day, and he sho' did hurt. He said I was bad, but when I got to be big I had to work. I had to keep the woodbox in the kitchen filled with wood, and I had to tote out the ashes. Then they made me sweep the stamp in front of the big house. They quit lettin' me pick up the eggs, 'cause I would slip some of the eggs out and hide them and get off and roast them eggs in ashes to eat.

One time when they set out little onion plants in the garden, I stole a piece of bread from the kitchen and slipped in the garden and pulled up lots of onions and ate them. When they missed them onions, they laid it right on to me, and I caught the whip hard.

My mammy was named Delilah, and she was the best cook in the world. Old Missus knowed it, and she kept her in that kitchen all the time. When big meetin' would come, my mammy would stack them cakes high up on the shelf in a big room. One time I slipped in there and pinched off a big piece of cake. They sho' whipped me that time. And another time I got my hand in a jar of jam and couldn't get it out. My mammy had to get it out for me, and I was whipped for that.

My pappy was named Jordan, and he work in the field and drove the team of oxen to Covin'ton, Louisiana, with a big wagon loaded with cotton—all that four yoke of oxen could pull at a time. He was always gone a week, and when he come back the wagon was filled with flour, and salt, and sugar. One time he brung a barrel of mackeral, and I stole some of that and was whipped again.

Ole Marse always brung back fine things for ole Missus, such as fine silk dresses, and fine hats, and shoes, and everything she wanted.

Everyday there was a big pail of milk put in a big trough in front of Mammy Lit's house, under a shed, for all of the little black chilluns to eat with bread in it. Every one of us had a spoon, and we would dip in to it and see who could get the most. Mammy Lit would beat me over the head and tell me not to be so greedy and eat it all from the others.

Marster's house was a big ole house and made of logs. It was two houses put together with a big hall and a shed room on both ends of the gallery. Then he covered that log house with plank. The plank was brung there from the Great Eastern sawmill, and my pappy hauled it with the ox team. That house had no paint on it, but when they covered it with plank they cut and put in glass windows. They had brick chimneys all the time. The water shelf was on the north end of the front gallery, and it had a shed built over it to keep the sun from gettin' the water hot.

Ole Marse had plenty mules, and goats, and cows, and chickens, and oxen, but only three horses. He thought more of them horses than he did of all the mules.

They seed the big war was comin' and said the South couldn't be beaten. Then one day ole Marse rode 'way on one of the fine horses, and ole Missus cried and cried and said he was gone and maybe get kilt. Some of the slaves wanted ole man Abe to whip the South, and some of them was for the South. One day I saw the Yankees comin' up the big road, and they asked my missus to give 'em somethin' to eat. She told them she had nothin'. They just went to the smokehouse and busted open the door and took all our meat and sugar and flour with them. They took the two fine horses that ole Marse loved, but they bothered nothin' in the big house, and ole Missus just cried.

Them Yankees went down to the gin and set fire to it with all the cotton and burnt it up. Then some of the slaves run 'way and went with the Yankees. They took two of ole Marse's mules, and they never come back.

One day old Marse come back home to stay, and he looked mighty sad. One day he rung the big bell and had all the darkies come to the house and told them they was freed. He told them if they would stay with him he would contract with them. Some of them left right then, and some of them stayed on. My mammy stayed on, and I stayed with her, and then ole Marse paid me for some work. But he paid me mighty little.

You know we had to shuck and shell corn and put it in big bags and put it onto mules. Some of us would get on top of that sack of corn and take it way down in Louisiana to a mill and bring back home the meal. I rode one of the mules and ole Tobe rode the other one. We was the one that went to the mill. We was gone all day.

After the war was over I stayed on with ole Marse nigh on to five years, and he couldn't pay me for my work. Then I went to the Eastern sawmill out from Osyka and hired to Joe Bridewell. He put me to skinnin' logs 'fore they was put to the saw. He give me a dollar a day, and I sho' was happy. I stayed at that mill and work for 'bout four years, when the mill burnt down.

I was married when I was a mighty young man—to

a bright girl named Josephine Williams, and she made me a good wife. She stayed with me 41 years and had seven chilluns. I couldn't read nor write, and she couldn't, but we sent all of our chilluns to school. When they got big enough to help us, they left home and went way up North and done forget us. My ole woman died 'bout 10 years ago, and I live with my sister, Lindy Brumfield, and her daughter, Nora Walker. They are good to me. I am too old to work, 'cept I try to make a garden.

My mammy, Delilah, lived to be 108 years old. She got so old she couldn't walk and had to set in a chair all the time, and somebody had to tote her in a chair whenever she went out of the house. She come to this country from Kentucky. Marse Edwin bought her from a man who was takin' a lot of slaves to New Orleans to sell.

I joined the Little Tangipahoe Baptist Church when I was a young fellow, and they turned me out for stealin'. Then they took me back. Then I went to preachin', and I sho' preached the Gospel for a long time. After a while, the members of that church quit payin' me, and then I quit preachin'. No use to preach when your members just spend all their money for whiskey and won't pay no parson.

My membership is now with Osyka Shiloh Baptist Church. Reverend Evans is the shepherd of the flock, and I's going to stay with them people 'til I pass on. I believe in shoutin', and I know when you get happy in the Lord you got a right to tell it.

I don't know nothin' 'bout Mr. Lincoln, but Mr. Roosevelt is mighty good to all the poor folks, for they tell me he is the man who sent us all the relief and help us poor niggers to live. I know Reverend Evans is the finest of them all. He is a good man, and the niggers don't pay him 'nough to preach.

I know there is spirits. I's seen 'em, and I done talk to the Lord 'bout 'em. One time I was comin' by the graveyard, and I seen a spirit. I seen them eyes shinin' like the sun. I said to it, "Who that there?" and it said nothin'. I said again, "Who that there?" and that time I chuck it with a stick. Then it made like it was comin' for me. Then I run, and the faster I run, the faster it run. I looks back, and I seen it comin'. Then I runs faster. It looked like a dog, but it was big as a mule. I hollered and I hollered. When I was near the house, I calls Josephine. She would not come, and I kept hollerin'. After a while I fell on the doorsteps and kept hollerin'. Then Josephine opened the door and asked, "What was the matter with me?" I kept hollerin' and couldn't tell her. After a while, she throwed cold water on me. Then I come to myself and told her 'bout the spirit. She said, "Go 'long nigger, you's just had too much liquor." I tell you, I never went by that graveyard again after dark.

Maria White

Age approximately 84 when interviewed
at her home in Coahoma County, Mississippi

Is you ever heard of a paralysis stroke? That's what they says struck me about sixteen years ago, and since that time I done lost my power in half of my body. I was born in the year 1853. The folks all say I don't know how old I is, and I don't. But I is certain I was born in the year 1853, 'cause my ma always kept up with it. She gave the number to me and told me don't never forget it.

My ma's name was Judai, and my pa's name was William. They didn't have but two children, me and my sister Hannah. We was both born on Mr. Low Fletcher's place near Koscuisko. Master Low was a mighty fine man. He treated us all good. He looked after his place hisself and didn't have no overseer or driver 'til the war broke out. Soon as that war started, Master Low joined the army. He was a captain in it. That kept him away from home all the time 'cept when he could slip away at night and come home to see his family. Master Low's wife, Miss Nancy, was the boss of things after master left. She got an overseer to see that the work went on. He was old poor-white trash, but he sure would do what Miss told him. He got the slaves up at the crack of dawn and worked them 'til dark.

Miss Nancy had six children when the war was over. I don't know how many she had after that. She took me in the house to learn me how to nurse the baby. She sure was a fractious lady. When I didn't do things to suit her, she would whack me over the head with whatever she had in her hand. I slept on the floor by the baby's crib. When she called me to get up, if I didn't hear her, she would throw a glass of water in my face no matter how cold the water was. You couldn't never leave the place unless old Miss gave you a pass to go. If you did leave, them patterollers would sure bring you back, and they wouldn't take no foolishness off nobody. One day Miss gave the order to have one of the women whipped. The next day Master came home. He sure got mad about that whipping. He said they was his slaves, they came from his folks, and he wouldn't stand for having nobody whip them.

Master's place wasn't very large, but it was big

enough to raise all the food we needed. Us had a garden, cows, and hogs. There was plenty of game such as possums, rabbits, and coons. Old Aunt Minta cooked for all the slaves. She fed all the children before night so they could rest well. My grandma, Charity, and my ma did the spinning of the thread and the weaving of the cloth. They had a big loom that the cloth was made on. Besides making the cloth for our clothes, they made it for the soldiers, too. They used dye to color the soldier's clothes, but ours was just left natural. We wore them same little slips in the winter that we wore in the summer. The hardest thing to get was shoes. They would buy them for the work hands in the winter, but us children had to go barefooted.

My owners was kinda young folks. They wasn't so rich, and the house they lived in wasn't nothing to brag on, but they was good.

I is heared my mother tell me many times about the slave dealers. She said they would take the slaves from place to place all chained together. They would make them sing to attract attention. Some of them would be crying 'bout leaving their children. Ma said my pa was put on a bench and sold just like stock would be. One day a dealer brought a big drove of slaves [to her plantation]. Among them was a real yellow nigger that could read and write. The folks wouldn't believe he was a nigger 'cause he could read and write. They wouldn't let that man stop there long. They kept him going. None of us had ever been taught anything in the way of book learning. We wasn't taught no Bible neither. The grownups could go to the white folks' church on Sunday, but they wouldn't let the children go.

I never heared of any trouble between the whites and coloreds. There was one man on the place named Henry. He was the terriblest fellow about running off. He had been caught many times by the patterollers and brought back. The last time he ran off, he went to the North, and we never seed that man again.

When we had our quilting parties, we invited our neighbors to come. Same way with dances on Saturday nights. Nobody better attend what ain't got no pass 'cause them patterollers is sure looking out for that. Everybody would tell the news they heared on their places as that was the only way we had for the word to get about. There wasn't much celebration on Christmas like there is these days. The children was given some cakes and candy, and that's about all there was to it. Maybe that's why we had so little sickness, as there wasn't all that trash to eat. Then too the children all wore asafitida bags around their necks, which helped to keep off diseases.

We didn't wear charms, and all such as that, like they do now. I never even heard about a hoodoo doctor 'til after the war. The only person that ever died was Old Aunt Minta and my pa. They was carried off the place somewhere to be buried, but I can't recollect much about it, 'cept that it was the second year of the war.

We often saw big regiments of Yankee soldiers passing by. Once when Master was home, some of them came on the place looking for him. They never did catch him. He always managed to dodge them somehow. I heard the old folks say the white folks tried to keep us from hearing about freedom. They couldn't keep that from our ears. There was so much talk going on. Quick as my ma heard it, she left that place and took me and my sister with her. Old Miss was in the bed with a young baby. None of us didn't so much as go near her to say good-bye, 'cause none of us didn't care if we never seed her again. We didn't get any land like we thought we was going to get, but we found a home on another big plantation, where they was in need of hands. I stayed there until I married Louis Jefferson. I had one child by him named Emma. She died when she was eleven months old, and I has never had no more children.

After my first husband died, I married Columbus White. He had one child, Lucille, when I married him. I is living with her now and has been ever since Columbus died. All my days I has done nothing but farm. You know how colored folks is about going here and yonder. Well, that's how we happened to come by the Delta, just changing about trying to better ourselves. I has lived here now sixteen years. I is a member of the Methodist church. Before I joined it, I was a Baptist, but confusion and one thing and another caused me to change. I still like that Baptist religion best of all. This younger generation that's coming on now sure is much better brought up than we was. They is got fine schools where they can get learning and nice brick churches where they hears the word of God. If they don't turn out right, there ain't no excuse for them. I sometimes wonders what I would have thought, when I was young, if I could have waked up some morning and seen the world just like it stands today.

Jake Dawkins

Age 92 when interviewed
at his home in Monroe County, Mississippi

I tell you, me and Marse Lige, that was Miss Emily's boy, was one-years chillun, and he tell me that us was born in eighteen and forty-five, so that would throw me being 'bout 92 years old, wouldn't it? Ain't many folks 'round, black or white, that is as old as I is. My first marster was old Joe Mays, but he give us all to his daughter, Miss Emily. He lived at Athens, and that was the time when it was the county seat. They had a jail and big courts and ever'thing. Miss Emily's husband was a Dawkins, but she done most of the bossin' 'fore he died, she and her paw (he lived with them).

My mammy and pappy was name Adeline and Jim Dawkins, and they come from the Carolinas. My mammy told me that when Marse Joe bought her, he paid five hundred dollars for her when she was put up on the auction block and sold.

Miss Emily had four boys and six girls. I warn't nothin' but a little fellow durin' most of slavery. Me and my three brothers and sisters used to play with the white chillun all the time. We used to play hide the switch and bugger bear. I never liked that bugger bear game 'cause it was right scary. When the one that was it would put smut or red berries on they face I'd run and hide and wouldn't come back 'til my mammy come after me. One night they didn't find me 'til after dark, and my mammy sho' wore me out.

We never had much chance to go to church durin' slavery times. The old marster wouldn't 'low the niggers to have no meetin's on his place. Some of the older folks would slip off sometimes and go over to the Gen'ral Davis's place that was next to ours. They had big meetin's there. The only time I 'member going to a meetin' was when the marster took all the slaves over to the white folks' church at New Hope and had a white preacher to preach to us. But Lord, he never did much preachin'. His text was, "Obey your marster and mistress," and he never told us a word about savin' our souls from hell and fire and damnation. Sometime when some of the niggers slip off to meetin's, the patterollers would catch them and give them thirty-nine lashes with they whips. The patterollers was a bunch of the meanest overseers from all the plantations 'round.

We had lots of young marryin's in those days. Old Marster would get a boy and a gal that had been walkin' together and tell 'em he's going to marry them. He take a paper and read some stuff off of it and then say, "Nigger, jump the broom!" And he'd make them both jump over a broom and then say they was married. That's the reason so many of the colored folks had been livin' together for a long time was married again after the Surrender by a preacher. They might not of had much sense but they knowed that warn't no right way to get married.

Old Marster liked fiddlin' and dancin', and that was one thing he 'lowed the niggers on his place to do. We'd have a big time 'til he'd go and get drunk and tell the overseer to whip everybody.

The only whippin's I ever got was from the mistress and from my mammy and they was alway 'bout fightin'. Miss Emily'd told all us chillun that she didn't want none of us to never tell a lie, and that she was going to whip us if we did. Whenever we's playin' and some of the other kids would say I was tellin' a story, I'd jump on them and start a fight. When Miss Emily'd come out to stop us and to whip us for fightin', I'd tell her I fought 'cause somebody called me a lie [liar], and I ain't never tell a lie 'cause she don't 'low that. Then she don't whip me so hard and sorta smile-like at me. She was a good woman and always was bringin' the chillun somethin' on Christmas, like candy and apples. She wouldn't 'low her daddy to whip us either.

When the war started I was a-workin' in the field, but Miss Emily took all the niggers to town to see Marse Lige go off to war. We went 'round to the place where they was drillin', it was where Judge Acker has his garden now, and I guess there was a million soldiers there. Marse Lige's colonel was named Gaines, I think. We had a right-hard time after that 'cause the Yankees come through and took all the stock. They stole Miss Emily's silver and took her money she had hid and then took all the nigger mens 'cept my daddy and another old man what was too old to go. The womens and us boys had to finish the crop that year. 'Bout two years after that, they brung young Marster home with a bullet in his shoulder, and they thought for a long time he might die. Miss Marthe, that was his sister, she lost her mind worryin' 'bout him and went plum crazy. From then 'til she died they had to keep somebody lookin' after her all the time, 'cause she was sho' crazier than a betsy bug!

We stayed on and helped Miss Emily that year and farmed third and forth with her—you know, the niggers get a third of the corn and a fourth of the cotton. My mammy and us chillun, my pa was dead then, cleared 'bout a bale of cotton and loads of corn that year. We moved to the Carlisle place the next year and stayed there for a right smart while.

I never married 'til I was 'bout thirty 'cause my mammy made such a racket 'bout leavin' her. Why, I 'member once when I was 'bout twenty I walked with a girl one Sunday. When I came home, Mammy made me take off all my clothes, and she wore me out. I is married three times, but all my wives is dead now, and I lives here with my daughter, Maria. She is mighty good to me, and we is good Christians. I joined the church 'bout two years after the Surrender, and I's been a faithful member ever since.

Don't the Good Book teach that there is two kinds of spirits, the evil and the good? And don't it say that the spirits is always with you? One time when I was on the way to church I step aside to let one [a spirit] by me. Annie, she was my wife then, she didn't have much faith in ghosts. She asked me what I was steppin' 'side for. I told her, and she laughed at me. But I did see him, and he was a big fellow without no head and with a white bosom. They won't bother you lessen you get in the way and lessen you do somethin' wrong. You know how I tells if I is going to meet one? I feels the warm streak of steam in the air. You 'member old man Burg? He used to have a big mill, and I worked for him. I was with him when he died. Fact was, he died with his head in my hand. Why, I seen him most every week, as plain as day. Ghosts can't talk, but I sho' wish they could, for I'd like to talk to that man.

I sho' would hate to meet old Marster on one of

these dark nights and him drunk—I's talkin' 'bout his ghost. I'd sho' strike out for the biggest stream of water in the country and get across as fast as I could 'cause, you know, ghosts can't cross water.

Fanny Smith Hodges

Age unknown when interviewed
in her home in McComb, Mississippi

My name's Fanny Hodges. I was Fanny Smith before I was married. My mammy was Jane Weathersby,
and she belong to old man Weathersby in Amite County.
He was the meanest man whatever lived. My pappy was
sold before I was born. I don't know nothin' 'bout him.
I had one sister—her name was Clara—and one
brother—his name was Jack. They said my pappy's name
was George. I don't know.

Mammy said when I was just big 'nough to nurse
and wash little chilluns, I was sold to Marse Hiram
Cassedy. That man give me to his daughter, Miss Mary,
to be her maid. The Cassedys sho' was good people. I
was big 'nough to draw water and put it in a tub and

wash Miss Mary, Miss Annie, and Miss July. I had to keep 'em clean. I had to comb they hair and they would holler and say I pulled. I was told not to let anything hurt them chilluns.

I slept in the quarters with the other niggers. Before sunup I had to get to the big house to dress them chilluns. I don't 'member what kind of bed I had, but reckon it was good. I ate in the kitchen. They fed fine. I ate what the white folks left, and sometimes they had possum and taters.

Marse Cassedy was a big judge. He went to all the courts and rode in a fine carriage with two big horses hitched to it, and a driver. He wore fine clothes and ever'body said he was a mighty big man. He had lots and lots of money. I don't know how many acres in his plantation but he had more'n 50 slaves.

When Marse Cassedy was gone, his overseer would be hard on the slaves, but Marse Cassedy would tell him not to be too hard. He never 'lowed his driver to draw blood when they whupped. He fed his slaves. They all had gardens, and he took care of us. He had money in every one of us. The overseers was white men workin' for wages.

I was never whupped after I went to Marse Cassedy. Slaves was whupped when they wouldn't work right. Sometimes they was lazy. The overseer blowed a horn every mornin', and the slaves knowed to get up. When that horn blowed again, they knowed they must go to the field. They blowed the horn at dinner and night.

After supper, we set 'bout and sing and go places. Sometimes the men would steal off and go to other plantations, and when caught they got a whuppin'. If the patteroller got 'em, they sho' caught it. They was whupped and brung back.

The white folks had big dances in the big house, and the niggers played the fiddle. They was fine times. They had good things to eat, and I always got some of what was left. Christmastime the slaves had dances. I could sho' shuffle my feet. Shucks, folks don't dance like that any more.

When slaves was sick, they sent to the woods and got roots and herbs to doctor 'em with. If they had runnin' off of the bowels, they got red-oak bark and boiled it and made 'em drink it. It's the best thing right now to cure runnin' off of the bowels. If young gals had pains in they stomachs they made tea out'n gum bark and that would bring 'em 'round. When babies was born, they had good midwives to wait on 'em. That was good money.

When Miss July got married, they had two cooks in the kitchen makin' pound cake for more'n a week, and pies, and chicken pie, and they killed a hog. They had ever'body in the country savin' butter and eggs for a long time. I didn't see the weddin', but the yard was full, and we had ever'thing to eat.

My folks was rich. Marse Cassedy went to the war, and he was a big man there. He was gone a long time.

They kept tellin' us the Yankees was comin', and Miss Fanny had her silver put in a bag and hid. They had the money put in a wash pot and buried, and they ain't found that money yet. When the Yankees come, they carried off all the meat in the smokehouse, and the blanket, and quilts, and ever'thing they wanted.

When Marse Cassedy come home he had the overseer blow the horn 'bout ten o'clock and told 'em all they was freed. He said he'd work 'em for wages, and nearly ever'one of 'em stayed for wages. I stayed with Miss Mary 'bout ten years. Then I married.

Me and Jake [Fanny's husband] went to Summit to live. We had to work mighty hard. Sometimes I plowed in the field all day. Sometimes I washed, and then I cooked. After 'while, we moved down to the new town. I come here when this town first started. I cooked for Mrs. Badenhauser, while he [Mr. Badenhauser] was mayor of the town. They worked me hard. Me'n Jake had some hard ups and downs. I had four chillun, none of them livin' that I know of. I might have some grandchilluns but if I do, they live up North.

I'm old and can hardly get about. I's got a cancer. The doctor done cut my left breast clear offen me but that hurts me sometimes yet. I gets a pension of four dollars a month, and I try to wash a little for the colored folks, and then I beg. I can't stay here long, but God won't 'low me to starve. Bless God, he's comin' for me some day.

Lucy Donald

Age unknown when interviewed
in her home near Puckett, Mississippi

My pa, he was sold and traded in Alabama and was brung here in Mississippi and sold with a bunch of other slaves. I don't know nothing 'bout my folks way back 'fore they was sold here and yonder and switched 'bout 'til I just knows I's got a pa and ma and that's 'bout all. I knows Marse Donald lived in Rankin County on a pretty-good-size plantation and owned several families of slaves. He bought my pa when my pa was just a young man. Pa hadn't been with him long 'fore pa married a strange woman named Lucy. She turned out to be my ma, and she, poor thing, died when I was just a week old. I was named Lucy for her. I wasn't took in and raised by the white folks like the most of 'em was when they was left like that. I was looked after by first one of the slaves, then another. I reckon I was kinda jerked up in the little log cabins 'round Marse's place. It seemed like colored folks didn't know the love and care of their chillun 'way back there, 'cause you see it was like this. They was first savages back in Africa and didn't know nothin' 'bout sticking together. When the white folks brung 'em over here, they snatched 'em up and sold and traded 'em away from one another. The chilluns was took away from their pas and mas. Husbands and wives was separated and sold.

Our cabins was little one-room huts built of logs with mud and straw chimneys. The chillun mostly slept on the floor on pallets in the wintertime and in the summer they slept mostly anywhere they dropped off to sleep. Sometimes it was on the piazza or on the grass, under the big trees or in the shuckhouse.

Now Marse's house was big and purty. It was a big two-story building. They had plenty of slave gals for servants and nurses. That place was kept spick-and-span and astir with all kinds of work going on. Slave men kept the grounds and gardens. There was always plenty fruit, vegetables, and the like a-growing. It sho' did take a heap to keep plenty for his big family and the slaves, too. Most ever'thing was growed and made right there on the plantation.

A big horn was blowed for signals. We all knowed what each blow meant. We knowed by the blows of the horn when to go to Marse's big kitchen to eat. Slave women cooked the food for everybody. It was set on long tables. The horn blowed for 'em to go to work, and to come in, and if a fire broke out. And we knowed what it meant by signals. The work was carried on from 'fore day 'til after dark. There sho' was a heap of work done in one day.

Ever'thing most and generally went on purty peaceful-like, but once in a while the overseers would get riled up with some of the slaves and whip 'em. If they got real stirred up, they would tie 'em to a tree and whip 'em. They [the slaves] sho' did dread them beatin's and knowed to mind what was said.

Now, while our mas was a-workin' in the fields, we little 'uns was sorta turned loose 'bout the place. The slave women that worked 'round Marse's house looked after us a bit. We was fed after the grown folks had got through eatin'. It warn't much to give us our food, as most of the time us was fed like little pigs, all in the same pan or big bowl. We ate mostly bread, 'lasses [molasses], meat, sweet taters, pot likker, and milk. Then we run 'round in the fresh air and sunshine and played as hard as we could at marbles, hopscotch, run-and-catch games, climbin' trees, gatherin' nuts, and playin' in the branch. Now, we could find plenty to do. Then when we got a little bigger, we was put to little jobs 'bout the place and then on to heavier work.

Back in them days, the darkies was superstitious and

easy scared up, and there the war was 'bout to fume up. They paid a heap attention to signs and things they seed. Most ever'thing pointed to something. I's gone with 'em to the woods to preach, and pray, and sing. They didn't want the white folks to hear 'em. Now, the pleasures [dances, parties, etc.] was the same way. They was carried on with a fear and superstition, always expectin' something to happen. I recollect one night, I was little but it's almost like it happen yesterday. The darkies was havin' a frolic in a old vacant house. This frolic was like all the rest of 'em, with dancin' by fiddle music, a-playin' "Turkey In the Straw" and "Molly Put the Kettle On." They would skip and play games. It got 'round close to midnight when things was likely to happen. Well, ever'thing was going purty when all at once a terrible-lookin' man with fiery eyes run fast as he could plumb through the crowd. He was a-shoutin', "Dance up, hogs, you ain't half a-dancin'." He run out through the back door and on into the woods. Part of the crowd nearly broke their necks a-jumpin' out of the windows a-gettin' away from there, while others believed they had to mind that ghost and went to dancin' for all they was worth. And when they did, the house caved in. I has wondered since then which was the best off—the ones that run scared to death out in the night or the ones that stayed.

Durin' the war was tryin' and troublesome times for us. The colored folks didn't know what was comin' next. The cavalrymen ridin' through lookin' for deserters and a-takin' what they could away from the folks in the way of food and good hosses. Sometimes we would see soldiers marchin' and hear guns a-shootin'.

When the Surrender come on and us was freed, the colored folks was adrift for a few years. They didn't know what to do. As they didn't know nothin' but to farm, they hired out to white farmers or homesteaded 'em some land. My folks worked on with Marse for a year or so and then homesteaded a tract of land and got to ourselves.

When I married it was like this. Elbert Jones was a good-lookin' nigger and went with any gal he wanted to. He was the popularist feller I ever seed. I was 'round nineteen years old, and he hadn't never paid no 'tention to me, he was so busy courtin' the rest of the gals. One day he come up to my house and say, "Lucy, why can't me and you get married?" I thought he was a-jokin', and I say back to him, "We is old 'nough." You see, I hadn't counted on him, so I just talked like that to be mannerly. He say, "I mean it." I say, "You know where yo' gal is at," and he say, "I sho' do." From then on we courted 'til we got used to each other, which took about three or four months. Then us married. 'Fore then I had courted boys for five or six years, but they won't like Elbert. We raised two chillun and give 'em some education. They lives on farms. Elbert has been dead a long time now.

Ruben Fox

Age unknown
when interviewed in Coahoma County

I was born in Washington County, Mississippi, south of Greenville. The place where I was born is now all gone down in the Mississippi River. I don't know what year I was born. I don't know how old I was when peace was declared, but I do know I was big enough to plough, so I must have been in the neighborhood of twelve or thirteen.

My master's name was Mr. June Ward, and his wife was Miss Matilda. The slave traders brought us from north, some place by the name of "Kentucky," and sold us to old Master. There was four of my family brought down together. My grandpa, Peter Lee, and his wife, Granny. That's the only name I is ever heard for my grandma. My father Ike, my mother Mandy, my brother West, my sister Minter, and me was all born after they came to Mississippi.

All the houses in the quarters where we lived was made of brick. Some says the brick was made right there on the place. I can't say as to the truth of that, 'cause I sho' ain't never seed no bricks made.

Master was real old when we came, and he didn't live so long. Mr. George, the oldest son, took charge of the place, and I always thinks of him as my master. There was two boys in the family, Mr. George and Mr. June. They didn't have no sister, so Mr. George was the boss.

The great big hall where everybody ate was called the cook kitchen. It was made of wood and whitewashed to look clean and nice. The old folks did the cooking, and they could sho' make things taste good. They took time with it and cooked them greens down as they should be. There wasn't all that hurrying like there is now. They knowed that as they finished one meal it would be 'bout time to start with another, so they didn't let that bother their minds.

When the grownups finished eating, the children was fed. Old Granny looked after that. She had big trays made of wood hollowed out to put the food in. She made me and the older children help her care for the little ones. We better not let none of them get hurt, I tell you that.

The biggest fun what the men had on the place was

going hunting. Game wasn't scarce like it is now, and they could keep the kitchen supplied with ever'thing, such as 'coons, possums, squirrels, and rabbits. Once I went hunting and killed a rabbit just as he was coming out of a hole in the graveyard. Everybody what ate a piece of that rabbit got sick. Whenever I wanted to make two bits, all I had to do was catch me a nice big terrapin. The white folks loved terrapin soup, and they would always buy them from me. All of us was allowed to keep any money we made.

Master George was mighty good 'bout giving us money whenever we asked him for it. We didn't have much need for money, so we very seldom asked for it. All our clothes was made and given to us. They even made the cloth they used with one of them spinning wheels. Our socks was knitted out of wool, and they sure did keep us good and warm. Our shoes was bought. I felt like I was the finest thing in the land when I got a pair of them boots with brass tips on the toes. There couldn't have been more than fifty or seventy-five head of slaves.

The old folks at the place made long shirts for us to wear in the summertime. We didn't wear nothing under them, but when winter came they made heavy wool underwear for us to put on under the shirts. They kept us good and warm.

Don't know as I ever heard them say how many acres there was in the place. It wasn't so powerful big, I knows that. Master George looked after it hisself. The big bell was in the yard. He rang it before day every morning for everybody to get up and out. I is knowed them to work as late as ten o'clock at night, when it was the light of the moon and they was behind with the cotton picking. There warn't no overseers or drivers. Them niggers was just natural good workers, and they didn't need none. Master sure didn't 'low no poor-white trash around there. It's them kind of folks what's got things so tore up now. This here young generation is the ones that let them in. The biggest thing the slaves got punished 'bout was fighting amongst theirselves. Boss tried to stop that and sometimes he would have to whip them 'bout it. He didn't always know when they fought, so there was mightly little punishment. There was so much to do on that place we didn't have time to get in much devilment.

The only person that ever ran off was my mother. She said she was going to try to make it to the free country. She didn't have no cause for leaving, 'cept she wanted to be free. She didn't get very far before them patterollers caught her and brought her back. That was the patterollers' business—to catch the folks what ran off and bring them back.

Besides making the crop, we had big herds of sheep and goats to be cared for, cows to be milked, and mules fed. When night came, we was ready to get in our beds and go to sleep. In cold weather we had hog killing.

Master's big smokehouse was so full of meat you couldn't see the top of it. The only Christmas we had was the hanging of the stockings by the children. They was filled with candy, cake, and apples. Saturday and Sunday was our rest days.

When we was sick, the old women made tea out of some kind of herbs that would cure any little ailment. For chills and fever old Master would issue medicine. He would give it to the old women, and they would give it to the sick person according to the way old Master said. We didn't know nothing 'bout wearing charms to keep off diseases. All such as that came up after the war.

The old folks called theirself teaching us religion. They 'lowed how we shouldn't have no rowdy bad doings, and they learned the children not to be sassy. The white folks would tell them to teach 'bout it being a grave sin to steal their chickens. There warn't no church on the place, neither for colored or white. We sometimes had little meetings in us houses and some old fellow preached much as he knowed, which was mighty little. We never had a baptizing, and I can't remember any funerals.

None of us could read or write. There was people in the country what did such as that on their place, but we didn't have it. The only way we had of getting news was by word of mouth. The slaves would go from place to place and tell what they heared. You never could put no 'pendence in what they told. Every time the news changed hands, it was told a little different. By the time it got to the end of the line, you wouldn't know it was the same story.

I is heared people all my life tell 'bout seeing haints and spirits, but I don't believe one word of it. They just thinks they sees them. I know I ain't ever seed even one, and I has lived much longer than them what tells those tales. I has seed many people depart this life what has been mistreated terrible, and if they don't come back to do something 'bout it, ain't nobody going to come.

It must have been nigh onto four years after the war was over before we heared about it. Master might have told us we was free, but I don't recollect it, 'cause that didn't mean nothing to us. We didn't want to go no-where. What us want to go for? Us was treated good, had ever'thing we wanted to eat and wear, and nice houses to live in, so we went right on making the crops same as ever. We didn't see nor hear nothing 'bout the war, and we didn't bother our minds with it. There might have been some promise made to the slaves on other places 'bout getting something when freedom come, but I is never heared of them getting nothing. We wasn't promised nothing. There wasn't no conversation 'bout it one way or the other.

I didn't know nothing at all 'bout Abraham Lincoln. I can recollect I is heard his name and that's all. The only thing I ever heard 'bout Jeff Davis was a song the folks sang. The words was "Going to hang Jeff Davis to a sour apple tree." There was another song they sang, too, about "Greely and Grant went up north. Greely stopped Grant, wearing broadcloth."

I never is been a hand to keep up with the time. I can't tell how long I stayed there, but it was many a long year. I married a woman named Sophia. We didn't hit it off so good, so I left her and married Liza. We lived together a right-smart time. I has been married to my present wife, Mary, over twenty years. I ain't never had no children that I knows of.

When I left Washington County, I came to Coahoma County and farmed on the Shacklefoot place and the Dorr place. Then I went to work for the high sheriff. That was a fine job. I looked after the courthouse, kept the yard, and fed the prisoners. My wife cooked the food, and I carried it to them. Besides that, I rented all them rooming houses in Foxes Alley, and run them, too. I sure did make plenty money. If it hadn't been for my ignorance, I would have saved some of it for my old age. Maybe the Lord thinks it right that I make it here and leave it here. I would have been working there yet if it hadn't been for this paralysis stroke what is going to carry me away from here.

I is a member of the Sanctified Church, and I don't let none of those hoodoo doctors worry me. If you follows the church's teaching, you will be right in your heart. The government give me old-age-assistance check every month. My wife takes in the washing to help care for me. She is a good woman. Heaps of young women like she is would have left me long ago. I 'spect the Lord arranged it that way, for all the goodness I done in my life.

Henrietta Murray

Age 84 when interviewed
at her home in Choctaw County, Mississippi

I was born here in Choctaw County, not more'n a mile from this place where I's livin' now. In all my life, I ain't never lived more'n three miles from where I's born.

My mama was Jane Roberson from South Carolina, and my papa was Daniel Roberson from South Carolina, too. My full brothers was Eddie and Wesley. After my papa's death, Mama married a Gladney fellow, and their chillun was Pamelia, Sammie, Sallie, Lucendy, Lucretia, and Laura. Wesley and I's the only ones livin' now. He lives over here on Biwy River and still tries to farm for a livin'.

My grandma come here from old Virginia, and I

never knowed my grandpa. She come here with her young mistress. She has told me her mistress was good to her.

I nursed in the Negro quarters durin' slavery days. All the colored women had to go to the field, and one old Negro woman stayed at the house to take care of all the little Negro babies. The biggest of us chillun had to help nurse the little ones.

We always had plenty to eat and clothes to wear, includin' shoes. They was a colored man on the plantation what made us brogans or "heel skinners" to wear. We had little log houses to live in and slept on home-made wheat or oat-straw beds.

Alex Roberson was our marster, and Missus Pamelia was his wife. That's who Mama named one of my sisters for. Marsa and Missus's chillun was Sarah, Martha, Necie, and Sammie.

Marsa always had a overseer on his place, but he wouldn't 'low 'em to hurt his Negroes. When one started mistreatin' slaves, he turned him off and got another one. I don't know how many slaves he had, but they was Uncle Lit, Jim, Anderson, Aunt Kissie and her chillun, Betsy and her brother, Aunt Patsy, and Aunt Nellie. That warn't all, but I just forgot the rest.

Our white folks didn't teach us to read and write befo' the Surrender, but my first teacher after the war ended was a white man. My grandma taught a Sunday school class on Sunday afternoons durin' slavery days and taught us all we knowed. We didn't have any church but had prayer meetin' and preachin' at our homes ev'ery Sunday evenin'.

The Negro women had to cook befo' daylight and after dark 'cause long as they could see they stayed in that field. Aunt Cendie cooked for the chillun.

The nurse women on the place handled most of the sick cases. The midwife waited on the women when the chillun was born unless 'twas somethin' special she couldn't handle. Then a doctor was called.

My papa come home from the Brest work with the measles and died. The other two chillun took 'em and died, too, but I never did take 'em.

After the war was over, our marsa come told us we was free by military laws. He didn't want us to leave, though. Most of the Negroes left, but befo' five years they was back.

When the Yankees come through old Marsa had us take Missus's saddlehorse and his two carriage horses to the woods. They went and got a barrel of sugar and flour, killed a cow, got heaps of chickens and hams. They eat what they wanted and left the other in the woods. Us chillun went to where camp was after they was gone and saw all the stuff they had left. We told our white folks, and they gathered it up and saved most of it.

The Ku Klux come to our house one night. We was livin' in half the house, and Uncle Jim in the other. They knocked on Uncle Jim's door and say: "Let me in." He say: "Who are you?" They say: "I'm Ku Klux." "Well, just stay out there then," he say. They all fell 'gainst the door and busted it open. Uncle Jim reached for his gun, and they struck him 'cross the hand. Out the door he went, and Auntie right behind him. Grandma followed 'em, but they saw her and grabbed her 'round the throat and led her back in the house. By that time I done got scared and crawled under the bed. They left then but took Uncle Jim's gun with 'em.

I think we had a better time when I growed up than young folks has now. We enjoyed bein' together. The young people now are more disagreeable than we was. When people fell out back then, they'd go together fist and skull. Warn't no such thing as killlin'.

We stayed with our white marsa two years after the Surrender, then went 'bout three miles south to a Mr. Taylor's and stayed 'bout two years. We went back to our white folks then and stayed on 'til he died. I married pretty soon after that and has been right here where I is for fifty-some odd years. I's always lived on a farm and ain't never knowed nothin' but hard work.

James Cornelius_____

Age approximately 91 when interviewed
at his home in Magnolia, Mississippi

I does not know the year I was borned, but they said I was fifteen years old when the war broke out, and they tell me I's past ninety now. They call me James Cornelius, and all the white folks says I's a good 'spectable darky.

I was borned in Franklin, Loos'anna [Louisianna]. My mammy was named Chlo, and they said my pappy was named Henry. They belonged to Mr. Alex Johnson, and whilst I was a baby my mammy, my brother Henry, and me was sold to Marse Sam Murry Sandell. We was brung to Magnolia to live, and I never remember seein' my pappy again.

Marse Murry didn't have many slaves. His place was

right where young Mister Lampton Reid is buildin' his fine house, just east of the town. My mammy had to work in the house and in the field with all the other niggers. I played in the yard with the little chilluns, both white and black. Sometimes we played "tossin' the ball," and sometimes we played "rap-jacket," and sometimes "ketcher [catcher]." And when it rained, we had to go in the house, and old Missus made us behave.

I was taught how to work 'round the house—how to sweep and draw water from the well, how to kindle fires, and how to keep the woodbox filled with wood. But I was crazy to learn how to plow, and when I could I would slip off and get a old black man to let me walk by his side and hold the lines.

Marse Murry didn't have no overseer. He made the slaves work, and he was good and kind to 'em. When they didn't do right he would whip 'em, but he didn't beat 'em. He never stripped 'em to whip 'em. He whipped me, but I needed it. One day I told him I was not goin' to do what he told me to do—feed the mule—but when he got through with me I wanted to feed that mule.

I come to live with Marse Murry 'fore there was a town here. There was only four houses in this place when I was a boy. I seed the first train that come to this here town. It made so much noise that I run from it. That smoke puffed out'n the top, and the bell was ringin'. All the racket it did make made me scared.

I heard them talkin' 'bout the war, but I didn't know what they meant. One day Marse Murry said he had joined the Quitman Guards and was goin' to the war, and I had to go with him. Old Missus cried and my mammy cried, but I thought it would be fun. He took me 'long, and I waited on him. I kept his boots shinin' so you could see your face in 'em. I brung him water, fed and curried his hoss, and put his saddle on the hoss for him. Old Missus told me to be good to him, and I was.

One day I was standin' by the hoss and a ball killed the hoss. He fell over dead, and then I cried like it might be my brother. I went way up in Tennessee, and then I was at Port Hudson. I seed men fall down and die; they was killed like pigs. Marse Murry was shot, and I stayed with him 'til they could get him home. They left me behind, and Colonel Stockdale and Mr. Sam Matthews brung me home.

Marse Murry died, and old Missus run the place. She was good and kind to us all, and then she married after a while to Mr. Gatlin. That was after the war was over.

Whilst I was in the war I seed Mr. Jeff Davis. He was ridin' a big hoss, and he looked mighty fine. I never seed him 'cept he was on the horse.

They said old man Abe Lincoln was the nigger's friend, but from the way old Marse and the soldiers talk 'bout him, I thought he was a mighty mean man.

I don't recollect when they told us we was freed, but I do know Mr. Gatlin would promise to pay us for our work and when the time would come to pay, he said he didn't have it and kept puttin' us off. We would work some more and get nothin' for it. Old Missus would cry, and she was good to us, but they had no money.

'Fore the war Marse Murry would wake all the niggers by blowin' a big "konk" [conch]. Then when dinnertime would come, old Missus would blow the konk and call them to dinner. I got so I could blow that konk for old Missus, but oh, it took my wind.

Marse Murry would 'low me to drive his team when he would go to market. I could haul the cotton to Covin'ton and bring back what was to eat, and all the oxen could pull was put on that wagon. We always had good eatin' after we had been to market.

Every Christmas I got a apple and some candy. Mammy would cook cake and pies for old Missus and stack them on the shelf in the big kitchen, and we had ever'thing good to eat. Them people sho' was good and kind to all niggers.

After the war the times was hard, and there was mighty little to eat. There was plenty whiskey, but I's kept away from all that. I was raised right. Old Missus taught me to 'spect white folks. Some of them promised me land, but I never got it. All the land I's ever got I work mighty hard for it, and I's got it yet.

One day after Mr. Gatlin said he couldn't pay me I run 'way and went to New Orleans and got a job haulin' cotton, and made my 50 cents and dinner every day. I sho' had me plenty money then. I stayed there might close onto four years. Then I went to Tylertown and hauled cotton to the railroad for Mr. Ben Lampton. Mr. Lampton said I was the best driver of his team he ever had 'cause I kept his team fat.

After I come back to Miss'ssippi, I married a woman named Maggie Ransom. We stayed together 51 years. I never hit her but one time. When we was gettin' married, I stopped the preacher right in the ceremony and said to her, "Maggie, iffen you never call me a liar, I will never call you one," and she said, "Jim, I won't call you a liar." I said, "That's a bargain." Then the preacher went on with the weddin'. Well, one day after we had been married 'bout four years, she asked me how come I was so late comin' to supper. I said I found some work to do for a white lady, and she said, "That's a lie." Right then I raised my hand and let her have it right by the side of the head, and she never called me a liar again.

My old lady had seven chilluns that lived to get grown. Two of 'em lived here in Magnolia, and the others gone north. Maggie is dead, and I live with my boy Walter and his wife Lena. They is mighty good to me. I owns this here house and four acres, but they live with me. I gets a Confed'rate pension of four dollars a month. That gives me my coffee and tobacco. I's proud I's a old soldier. I seed the men fall when they was shot but I was not scared. We ate bread when we could get it, and if we couldn't get it, we done without.

After I left Mr. Lampton, I's come here and went to work for Mr. Enoch at Fernwood when his mill was just a old rattletrap of a mill. I work for him 45 years. At first I hauled timber out'n the woods and after a while I hauled lumber to town to build houses. I sometimes collect for the lumber, but I never lost one nickle, and them white folks says I sho' was a honest nigger.

I lived here on this spot and rode a wheel to Fernwood everyday, and fed the teams and hitched 'em to the wagons. I was never late and never stopped for anything, and my wheel never was in the shop. I never 'lowed anybody to prank with it. That wheel was broke up by my gran'chilluns.

Afer I quit work at the mill, I's come home and plow gardens for the white folks and make some more money. I sho' could plow.

I joined the New Zion Baptist Church here in Magnolia and was baptized in the Tanghipoa River one Sunday evenin'. I was so happy that I shouted, me and my wife both. I's still a member of that church, but I's do not preach and I'm not no deacon. I's just a bench member and a mighty poor one at that. My wife was buried from that church.

When I was a young man, the white folks' Baptist Church was called Salem. It was on the hill where the graveyard now is. I went possum hunting in that grave-yard one night. I took my ax and dog 'long with me. The dog, he treed a possum right in the graveyard. I cut down that tree and started home, when all to once somethin' run by me and went down that big road like lightnin', and my dog was after it. Then the dog come back and lay down at my feet and rolled on his back and howled and howled. Right then I knowed it was a spirit. I throwed down my possum and ax and beat the dog home. I tell you that was a spirit—I's seed plenty of 'em. That ain't the only spirit I ever seed. I's seen 'em a heap of times. Well, that taught me never to hunt in a graveyard again.

Another time I was goin' by the graveyard, and I seed a man's head. He had no feet, but he kept lookin' after me and every way I turned he wouldn't take his eye offen me. I walked fast, and he got faster. Then I run, and then he run. When I got home I just fell on the bed and hollered and hollered and told my old lady. She said I was just scared, but I's sho' seed that spirit, and I ain't goin' by the graveyard at night by myself again.

Susan Jones

Age 95 when interviewed
at her home in Panola County, Mississippi

I was born on Mr. Charles Alexander's plantation in Panola County. My father and mother was Si and Easter Alexander. When the war broke out, I was not big enough to work in the fields, so I played in the yard and helped in the house. Both my parents died before freedom was declared.

After the war, I stayed with my brothers on the place for two years. All the slaves rejoiced, and most of them broke up and went to Memphis. When they found they couldn't get no work and live in the city, they all come back. We all started one Sunday morning and walked to Hernando and stayed all night under some plum bushes and walked to Memphis the next day.

I didn't see no fighting but just heaps of fighting soldiers from both sides. One Sunday morning early, the Yankee soldiers come through and set the public blacksmith shop on fire and took all the hosses, meat, and chickens they could find, and even got in the milk cellar and drunk all the milk.

All the slaves was fed just what the white folks ate, and it was plenty good. Marster Charlie Alexander was a poor man, and he married Miss Jane Byrd, who owned all the slaves and land. She wouldn't let him treat us mean, but when she died, he raised cain. He beat up all the slaves. Most any time you could hear niggers praying and hollering down at the neighbors' house. He whupped 'em just 'cause he could.

Why, he'd take them in droves down to the city and sell 'em just 'cause he didn't like 'em. He'd put 'em in the cattle pen 'til he sold them. My brother Henry Clay ran off in the woods after he whupped him so hard. He ran all day, and the white folks set the coon dogs after him, and he was caught. They put him in a barrel with a stick nailed over his shoulder and one between his knees, so as he couldn't get out. They put him in the yard so everybody could see him. Henry had a knife, so he whittled the stick and got out and run off again. After that, he was caught and whupped. The next time he run off, he joined the Union soldiers.

After Miss died, we had a overseer, and he sho' was poor-white trash, and a meaner man never lived. He and his family lived on the place, and the niggers warn't no more than dogs on our place.

I heard lots about the Klan, but I never did see 'em. They never done nothing to us. We didn't expect so much from freedom, but anything was better than what we had.

I can remember when Abraham Lincoln was running for the presidency. I've heard lots about him and seen Jeff Davis's soldiers and Lincoln's soldiers come through. They burned all the fine houses and smokehouses, and the white folk hid the silverware.

There was a man who come through, and he looked just like a tramp. Well, he inquired around the way and counted all the plow hands—we had fifteen plow hands and thirty hoe hands. The next day, the ground was darkened with soldiers. They asked where the plow hands was, and my cousin Paul said there warn't none. "Well," said the Yankee, "who runs them fifteen plows?" And Paul led them soldiers right down to the field, and they took all the mules and nigger men and made the men fight. Some of them deserted, and the others fought in the war. The man what had come the day before was a spy.

My husband, Simon Jones, fought in the war. He was in the Northern army under General Foster in Company K, Regiment 59. He was in the battle of Vicksburg and Gettysburg.

I ain't never seen no haints but I've heard 'em plenty

of times. I was walking in the house, and I thought it was my sister. I called, but she didn't answer and just kept on walking. So I went in and looked high and low, but there warn't nobody there. When I started out the door, it started again. My hair began to creep off my head, and I nearly broke my neck getting to the white folks' house. We would stay in the house with the white girls after they father died, and lots of times we would hear the piano playing, and they didn't have no piano. But you could hear them keys just a-playing, and folks would walk up and down the stairs.

Miss loved pretty things, but they just had common things and lived in a double log house. She begged for a safe and real china dishes, but he [her husband] wouldn't get 'em for her. But just after she died, he bought the safe and dishes. Night after night them dishes would rattle and shake, and we'd look and there was no one. The marster said it was cats, but we didn't have no cats. We just knew it was Miss. She rattled them dishes 'til every one was broke.